CW00375958

Realising
Your Full
Potential

Yan Hadley

New Life Publications

New Life Publications
45 Heatherbrook Road
Anstey Heights
Leicester LE4 1AL
Tel: 0116 2356992

Copyright © 1999 Yan Hadley

All rights reserved. No part of this publication may be reproduced,
stored in any retrieval system, or transmitted, in any form or by any
means, electronic, mechanical, photocopying, recording or otherwise,
without the prior permission of the publisher.

Short extracts may be used for review purposes.

Unless otherwise stated all Scripture quotations are from the Revised
Standard Version of the Bible. Copyright © 1946, 1952 by the division
of Christian Education of the National Council of the Churches of Christ
in the United States of America.

A V- Authorised Version. Crown copyright.

NIV- The Holy Bible, New International Version. Copyright © 1973,
1978, 1984 by International Bible Society.

ISBN: 0 9531107 1 0

Printed & Produced by: Moorley's Print & Publishing,
Published by: Newlife Publications, Leicester
23 Park Road, Ilkeston, Derbys DE7 5DA
Cover Design Concept by: Dryden Henderson

Dedication

This book is dedicated to the team who so faithfully have been working with me in the ministry of open-air preaching in the centre of Leicester.

Their commitment and enthusiasm has been a tremendous encouragement to myself, and also has brought great strength to an aspect of evangelism that is at times quite hazardous, and not well supported.

Not least among these workers is my good friend John Fairbairn, who for many years has worked together with me, both on crusades, and weekends of outreach. His glad and faithful involvement has been gratefully appreciated.

Contents

Acknowledgements

My grateful thanks go to my wife Lorrainne, for all her help and support in the hard work of typing the manuscript.

Much appreciation is also due to Pat Allen, in Leicester, Helen Cockram, in Cheshire, Jo Fraser, in Hertfordshire and Hazel Roberts, in Lancashire. Their diligence in the difficult task of proof reading the text has been extremely valuable.

Introduction

On a plaque in America, marking Abraham Lincoln's birth place near Hodgeville, Kentucky, there is recorded this scrap of conversation:

"Any news down t' village, Ezry?"

"Well, Squire Mclains's gone t' Washington t' see Madison swore in, and ol' Spellman tells me this Bonaparte fella has captured most o' Spain. What's new out here, neighbour?"

"Nuthin', nuthin' a'tall, 'cept fer a baby born t' Tom Lincoln's. Nothin' ever happens out here."

How wrong we can be about the potential of an individual life! What looks to have small beginnings and appear of no apparent significance can grow and develop into something far beyond our wildest imagining. This is the potential of the individual that we should never underestimate in others or ourselves.

Whoever would of thought that the man who could write the *Second Inaugural Address*, regarded by many as the noblest of all political documents, and the *Gettysburg Address*, had no more than four months of formal education, and that in a one-room country schoolhouse where students ranged from age five to twenty-five.

When Abraham Lincoln was seven years old, his family was forced out of their home on a legal technicality, and he had to work to help support them. At age nine, his mother died. At twenty-two, he lost his job as a store clerk. He wanted to go to Law school, but his education was not good enough.

In 1831, he failed miserably in business. The following year he was defeated for the legislature and then failed again in business a year later. In 1835 his fiancée died and in 1838 he was defeated for Speaker of the house.

Eventually, in 1842, he married into what historians call a "living misery" and only one of his four sons lived past the age of eighteen.

At thirty-seven, on his third try he was elected to Congress, but two years later, he failed to be re-elected. At forty-five, he ran for the Senate and failed. At forty-seven, he failed as the vice-presidential candidate and at forty-nine, he ran for the Senate again and lost.

In spite of all these set-backs though, he was elected as the 16th President of the United States and took the oath of office on March 4th 1861, at the age of fifty-two. By many today this man is still considered the greatest leader America has ever had.

The book you are about to read starts on the basis that each and every one of us have a destiny to fulfil. The life that we have been given is a gift from God, full of incredible potential, and we have a responsibility to find out what that destiny is and live our lives to the full for His glory.

We are followers of the one who *"Set His face as a flint to go towards Jerusalem."* Jesus, against all the odds, and in the knowledge of great personal hardship, determined to fulfil God's will for His life, even though this meant crucifixion and death.

Determination alone will not be sufficient to realise our full potential. It is for this reason that throughout each chapter of the book our mind in set firmly upon God's word, presenting clear spiritual principles. As we seek to apply these, putting them into practice in our daily experience, then His rich anointing will be upon us to make available what would otherwise be beyond our reach.

Chapter 1

Destined For Greatness

For years many people felt that running a mile in less than four minutes was impossible. Articles published in journals of physiology 'proved' that the human body just could not do it. Then on May 6th 1954, in Oxford, Roger Bannister broke the four minute mile barrier and within two years, ten others had also done the same. For more than a year the slender, sandy-haired medical student had trained relentlessly to be the first athlete in history to reach this goal.

The achievement and greatness that can be realised in the physical world is passing and lasts only for a short time, but what we can accomplish in the spiritual realm lasts for eternity. If our heart is set on living for the Lord, then no obstacle or barrier can prevent us from being all that God wants us to be. Locked up within every Christian is a tremendous wealth of potential that the Lord desires to see released for His glory.

God's word always comes to encourage us to be all that we have the potential of being. Even when it brings correction and discipline it expresses the heart of a father who wants to see his children grow into maturity and develop to be like him. The extent of the greatness we are destined for is described as, *".... to mature manhood, to the measure of the stature of the fullness of Christ."* (Ephesians 4:13b). This is the goal we should aim towards, even though at times we may feel far from it.

When Paul wrote to the Church at Corinth, he was aware of their carnality and unrighteousness but he reminds them, *"We have this treasure in earthen vessels...."* (2 Corinthians 4:7). Too often we get preoccupied with the apparent ordinariness of our lives; so aware of the

11

frailty and weakness of the *"earthen vessel"* that we forget about the incredible treasure which God has deposited within every one of us. We look at our flaws and weaknesses and neglect to focus on the treasure of God's life and power within.

It would seem to be part of human nature for some people to underestimate what they are able to do, while others push beyond the barriers and overcome whatever hindrances are trying to hold them back. One American advice columnist illustrated people's ability to overcome obstacles when she wrote:

> *"Cripple him and you have a Sir Walter Scott; lock him in prison and you have a John Bunyan; afflict him with asthma as a child and you have a Theodore Roosevelt; make him play second fiddle in an obscure South American orchestra and you have a Toscanini; deny her the ability to see, hear and speak and you have a Helen Keller."*

The glorious truth found in the scriptures is that because of the treasure we have within us, no one has to be a loser, or less than God intended! This fact is the clear conviction of my heart and the substance of this book, so let us consider right at the outset, four steps based on John 15:1-17, that enable us to walk as though we are destined for greatness:

Firstly, DETERMINE TO FULFIL YOUR DESTINY
Here is where greatness in God's sight begins. We must first believe that we have a destiny, that there is a point to our existence! We have no business muddling around in a fog of confusion and uncertainty. Instead, there ought to be a sense of destiny burning deep within our spirits that we are determined to fulfil. This destiny is what Jesus was referring to in verse 16 when He said, *"You did not choose me, but I chose you and appointed you that you should go and bear fruit and that your fruit should abide ...... "*

One of the greatest discoveries that we could ever make is that we have been chosen by almighty God. This is true not just for the missionary, pastor, evangelist or full-time worker, but also for every born-again believer.

If you listen to some Christians today giving their testimony, they often talk of how they 'chose' the Lord. In fact some speaking in this way give you the very distinct impression that they almost did God a favour when they decided to 'choose' Jesus! However, the truth is that we did not choose Him, He chose us. Also, equally as exciting as this, is the fact that we have been 'appointed' as well. There is a divine purpose in that choosing, an appointment which each one of us has to fulfil. God has called us not just to get by with a survival mentality but to be fruitful in every area of our lives. For this to become a reality in us we need to see beyond **'who'** and **'where'** we are at the moment, to what God wants us to **"be"** and **"do"**!

> Our Destiny in **'Being'** is seen in Ephesians 1: 4-6. Here it says,
> *"He chose us in Him before the foundation of the world, that we should be holy and blameless before Him. He destined us in love to be His sons through Jesus Christ, according to the purpose of His will."*

It is far beyond our ability to comprehend, but before this world was ever created we were already chosen by God to walk in a pure, holy, and righteous way. Again this is stated by Paul in Romans 8:29, *"For those whom He foreknew He also predestined to be conformed to the image of His Son...."* Our destiny is to be like Jesus; that in itself is greatness!

When we consider the imagery of the branch abiding in the vine that Jesus spoke of, we are reminded that God's word tells us, *"He who says he abides in Him ought to walk in the same way in which He walked."* (1 John 2:6). We ought to because it is our destiny; to walk with that same anointing, authority, sense of purpose, fruitfulness and that same purity of life. We are certainly not there yet, but the important thing is that we have the same attitude of determination which was expressed by Paul when he said, *"Not that I have already obtained this or am already perfect, but I **press on** to make it my own, because Christ Jesus has made me His own."* (Philippians 3:12). And again at the end of verse 13, when Paul refers to the effort involved in pressing on he speaks of, *"... ... straining forward to what lies ahead."*

This was not struggling in his own strength, nor striving in his own ability; rather it was a determination to lay hold of what he himself had been laid hold of by God for. He was committed to fulfilling his destiny!

Our Destiny in **"Doing"** is the work and area of service that God has appointed for us. Ephesians 2:10 says, *"For we are His workmanship, created in Christ Jesus for good works, which God prepared beforehand, that we should walk in them."*

Before we were even converted, long before we were a part of the Church, God had already prepared the area of ministry and service that He wanted us to function in. We just have to find out what this is and be fruitful in that calling. In some measure it might be what we are already doing, but there is an inner awareness that there's so much more still to come out of our gifting. On the other hand it might be a completely new direction that God has for us that we've not yet moved into, and there's a stirring that we are being led out of what we're doing and into something new. Whatever the case might be, the principle that will enable us to maximise our potential is found in the wisdom of Solomon. He said, *"Whatever your hand finds to do, do it with all your might; ...."* (Ecclesiastes 9:10).

The spirit of this age is one of apathy and half-heartedness, expressing the attitude of either, *"I can't be bothered"* or, *"any old thing will do."* In the Church however, we must have a different spirit. If we are to fulfil our destiny before God, then we need a spirit of excellence in all that we do. It is when we are faithful in the small things that we grow and the Lord will then appoint us to be faithful over much.

THE IMPORTANCE OF VISION

In August 1963 the civil rights leader and Baptist minister, Dr Martin Luther King Jr. stood up in Washington and declared, not just to America, but to the world, those now immortalised words, *"I have a dream."* This dream was to see an end to racial hatred and segregation between black and white. It was a dream for all people everywhere to be valued and treated alike, regardless of the colour of their skin. This wasn't the wishful thinking of his own vain imagination, but a strong God-given conviction gripping his heart that he was willing to sacrifice everything for. It was a cause that would consume him and, at the age of thirty nine, ultimately cost him his life!

A sense of destiny is always borne out of vision. To maximise our potential, vision is crucial. We read in the scriptures *"Where there is no vision, the people perish...."* (Proverbs 29:18, AV). Something dies within us if we have no vision to direct, motivate and guide our lives. A good paraphrase of this verse that I heard recently is,
> *"Where there are no plans and goals based on God's word, then people will drift into a meaningless, pointless, ineffective existence."*

If we are simply living for today with no thought for the future, then our lives will drift by with little achieved. Vision is essential for survival. It is spawned by faith, sustained by hope, sparked by imagination and strengthened by enthusiasm.

Whatever God plants in our spirits must be followed through by a determination to see it fulfilled.

Secondly, **DECIDE TO MAKE RADICAL DECISIONS**

It is one thing to have a sense of destiny, but quite another to be prepared to pay the price tag that is attached to this. If we are to see any breakthrough, and make any advance, it will always be incredibly costly. To see anything worthwhile fulfilled will demand great sacrifice. In our personal life we will need to make radical decisions about how we live. This is why Jesus said, *".... the Kingdom of heaven has been forcefully advancing and forceful men lay hold of it."* (Matthew 11:12, NIV).

Nothing less than single-minded, wholehearted, totally committed Christian living is required. This means seeing the Kingdom of God extended as the one cause worth living for and ruthlessly rejecting every distraction which conflicts with that.

15

History gives a good example of somebody who recognised the need to make radical decisions if advance and victory were to be established. When Julius Caesar landed on the shores of Britain, he ordered his men to burn every boat in which they had crossed the Channel. Then he marched them all to the edge of the cliffs of Dover and instructed them to look down. Seeing their boats engulfed in flames, they realised that he had cut off any possibility of retreat back to the Continent. There was now only one thing left for them to do, and that was to advance and conquer, and that's exactly what they did!

We also need to burn our boats, making no contingency plan for failure, just in case God's word doesn't work, or things don't turn out as we had hoped they would. There must be only one direction to our lives and that is to advance and conquer! The old chorus puts it so well with the words, *"I have decided to follow Jesus, no turning back, no turning back."*

DESTINY INVOLVES RIGHT CHOICES

What must be understood is that destiny comes not through chance, but through choice. Each one of us makes decisions every day that determine the course, quality, and effectiveness of our lives. That decision process to fulfil our destiny began the moment we made our first commitment to Christ, but it continues on, day by day, and will ultimately govern where we end up. A friend of mine that I worked with for several years is a solemn reminder to me of this. He had a very fruitful and respected ministry throughout this country, and in several nations abroad. Sadly though, the last I heard of him, he was a convicted prisoner in Rochester Prison.

The crime that he was sentenced for was very serious. It came out of a long-term problem that went back many years. The issues involved could all have been dealt with and resolved if only wrong choices had not been made by him. Even when I confronted him about his sin, long before his arrest and conviction, he chose to vehemently deny that anything was wrong. Rather than face up to his problem he chose to deceive others and live in deception himself. The wrong choices he made affected not only those that he'd directly sinned against, but also his marriage, family, reputation and ultimately his 'calling.'

The most important, life-changing decision we will ever make once we've become a Christian is found in the words of Jesus when He says, *"If you abide in me, and my words abide in you, ask whatever you will and it shall be done for you."* (John 15:7). This single word *"If"* which occurs throughout the chapter, speaks of a choice and will have a huge influence upon every area of our lives. No less than ten times in six verses Jesus tells us to *"abide in Him"*. To abide in Christ means there can be nothing in our lives that is contrary to Christ's nature, and for His word to abide in us means there can be nothing in our lives that contradicts His word. When we look at our daily living like this, then it becomes a great challenge to us. Disregarding this one single instruction is, I believe, the cause of all our unreached potential, unfulfilled desires, unresolved problems, unsettled emotions, and unanswered prayers!

The key that unlocks our potential for greatness is found in the choice of obedience that the word *"if"* confronts us with. This is also seen in the words of Moses when he addressed the people of Israel:
> *"And if you obey the voice of the Lord your God, being careful to do all His commands which I command you this day, the Lord Your God will set you high above all the nations of the earth. And all these blessings shall come upon you and overtake you, if you obey the voice of the Lord your God. Blessed shall you be in the city, and blessed shall you be in the field. Blessed shall be the fruit of your body, and the fruit of your ground, and the fruit of your beasts, the increase of your cattle, and the young of your flock. Blessed shall be your basket and your kneading trough. Blessed shall you be when you come in, and blessed shall you be when you go out. The Lord will cause your enemies who rise against you to be defeated before you; they shall come against you one way, and flee before you seven ways. The Lord will command the blessing upon you in your barns, and in all that you*

17

undertake; and He will bless you in the land which the Lord your God gives you. " (Deuteronomy 28:1-8).

Thirdly, DEAL WITH EVERYTHING DAMAGING TO FAITH

There are many things that get in the way and act like a blockage, stopping us from receiving what God so willingly wants to give. We need to let God get rid of all unnecessary restrictions in our lives; that is anything hindering us from developing into all that we could be. This is where verse two in John 15 becomes so important. Here Jesus says,

"Every branch of mine that bears no fruit, He takes away, and every branch that does bear fruit He prunes, that it may bear more fruit. "

Notice in this verse that nobody escapes! Those people doing well, and who have produced fruit are pruned by the Lord that they might bear even more fruit. Those that have areas of their lives not flowing with the life of God, He will prune and cut away that new life might flow. This 'pruning' comes in various ways. Sometimes God cuts away and prunes by the direct conviction of the Holy Spirit and sometimes through other people who might challenge us. On occasions this pruning will happen as doors close and barriers that God has put there hinder us.

Also this can occur as God allows our lives to experience periods of difficulty. Going through pain is part of the process of reaching our full potential. This is why James says,

"Count it all joy, my brethren, when you meet various trials, for you know that the testing of your faith produces steadfastness. And let steadfastness have its full effect, that you might be perfect and complete, lacking nothing. "

(James 1:2).

A good example of this is a mother and son that I met at Pontefract. The mother came to me at the end of the meeting and said,

"Yan, I agree 100% with what you've taught on how God can use pain to fulfil His purpose in us. We have gone through the most awful time over the last three years. My son has

18

suffered from severe and deep depression and has had two nervous breakdowns. He's tried to commit suicide on two occasions and has spent a short time in a psychiatric hospital. However, I can honestly say to you tonight that my son is a better person for having gone through those awful things that he did. Before, he was so hard and arrogant. He was indifferent and insensitive to others, but now he's a changed person. There is a gentleness and sensitivity to other people's problems that he never had before."

Now I am not suggesting that God sends pain and heartache to us, but because He is Lord, then even that which Satan intends for evil God is able to turn and work for good. Whichever way the 'pruning' comes, we need to recognise what the hindrances are and let God deal with them. Some of these things could be:

(A) *Lack Of Love*
God says in His word,
> *".... he who does not love his brother whom he has seen, cannot love God whom he has not seen."* (1 John 4:20).

When there is criticism, gossip, resentment, selfishness, indifference, etc., it hinders our destiny of being like Jesus and it also affects our relationship with God. This is why His word says, *"Whenever you stand praying, forgive, if you have anything against anyone; ...."* (Mark 11:25). It is for this reason, when Jesus was talking about fruitfulness, that He twice referred to love. In John 15:12 we read, *"This is my commandment, that you love one another, as I have loved you."*

And again in verse 17, *"This I command you, to love one another."* Unity is powerful and productive. The Devil knows that a united people will have the potential to fulfil their destiny and make an impact on their community, so he will try anything to spoil and disrupt relationships.

(B) *Sinful Habits*
We have a course that has been set for us by God, and a race to run. The only way that we can make sure of doing the best we can is when everything that might trip us up, or slow us down, has been removed from our lives. This is what the writer to the Hebrew Christians was

referring to when he wrote, *".... let us lay aside every weight, and sin which clings so closely, and let us run with perseverance the race that is set before us."* (Hebrews 12:1).

If our heart in any sense feels guilty and condemned it will affect our confidence before God and can also prevent us receiving all that He wants to pour into our lives. This is why the apostle John encouraged those he wrote to by saying,

> *"Beloved, if our hearts do not condemn us, we have confidence before God; and we receive from Him whatever we ask, because we keep His commands and do what pleases Him."* (1 John 3:21&22).

To receive from God we need to walk in righteousness and have a heart that is clean before Him.

(C) *Double-Mindedness*

When we have two minds about something it will bring instability to our lives and will stop us walking in the blessing that God wants us to know. We are being double-minded when we are thinking things like, *"Is that scripture for today or was it just for then?"-"Will God answer my prayer or perhaps I'm not praying for the right thing?"-"Is God going to use my life in the way that He uses other people?"*

This lack of confidence throws us into a state of insecurity. In fact the Bible speaks about how seriously this affects every area of our lives by using very firm words. It says,

> *".... He who doubts is like the wave of the sea, blown and tossed by the wind. That man **should not** think he will receive **anything** from the Lord; he is a double-minded man, unstable in **all** he does."* (James 1:6-8, NIV).

We must always approach God with a single-minded certainty to secure His promises.

(D) *Negativity*

Some people seem to be naturally negative. They allow their old way of thinking and speaking to influence their new nature. It is one thing to be positive in the congregation of God's people, where there is an atmosphere of faith and mutual encouragement, but it is something quite different in the pressures of every-day life. If we have a negative view of ourselves and what God will do for us, then our expectation of developing into our full potential is immediately dwarfed. Many people find themselves imprisoned like this because they just do not expect their situation is ever really going to change.

Negativity not only hinders us from achieving, it keeps us from being and prevents us from receiving. In James 4:2b we find one of the shortest, simplest and most straight forward statements in the Bible, it says, *"You do not have, because you do not ask."*

In over twenty years of full time ministry, I have met many hundreds of people who have robbed themselves by their negativity. Their expectation had become so low because of disappointment and discouragement, that they didn't bother asking anymore. They just did not expect God's promises to work for them, as they did for others.

(E) *Wrong Motives*
This will always be a major hindrance in our lives. Behind everything that we do and all that we pray for there is a motive; a reason why we do it. Sometimes we do things for the glory of God and blessing of other people and on other occasions we are motivated by our own selfish ends and self-centred reasons. When our motives are not pure it hinders us receiving what we need. The Bible says, *"You ask and do not receive, because you ask wrongly, to spend it on your passions."* (James 4:3).

Fourthly, DEVELOP AN ATTITUDE OF DARING
The old motto of the S.A.S. is, I believe, very appropriate for every Christian. It says, **"He who dares, wins"**! This is how we grow in our faith and experience. If we are to see ourselves moving toward greatness, then we need to get out of the boat of our security and be prepared to take a few risks. Stepping beyond where we are at the moment and having an attitude of daring keeps us from settling down and becoming complacent. Moving into new areas and doing things that we have never done before takes courage, but results in new discoveries and produces a richer experience of having proved God.

The encouragement that was given by the Lord to Joshua as he pressed in to discover the promised land holds just as true for us today. God said,

> *"Have I not commanded you? Be strong and of good courage; be not frightened, neither be dismayed, for the Lord your God is with you wherever you go."* (Joshua 1:9).

Hudson Taylor, the great missionary to China once said,

> *"Many Christians estimate difficulty in the light of their own resources, thus they attempt very little and they always fail. The real giants have all been weak men who did great things for God because they reckoned on His power and His presence to be with them."*

One of the most thought-provoking questions we could consider is, ***"When was the last time you did something for the first time?"***

This is not just an interesting play on words, it is a serious consideration for us all to not simply remain in the safety of what we've always done, or been used to, but to move on. We need to rise to the challenge of what the Bible says is possible for each one of us, and allow ourselves to be stretched.

Take the simple rubber band for example; they all work on the principle of needing to be stretched to be effective. In the same way, every person who has ever achieved anything for God has had to learn the same thing. Only when we are prepared to be stretched to meet challenges, do we find ourselves developing. No doubt we will make a few mistakes in the process, maybe even look a little foolish at times, but we can be sure God will always honour those who seek to honour Him in their lives.

Jesus gives two remarkable promises about our potential that are designed not just to encourage us, but to stretch us. He says,

> *"All things are possible to **him** who believes."* (Mark 9:23).

And also,

> *"…. nothing will be impossible to **you**."* (Matthew 17:20b).

Jesus wasn't speaking of what God was able to do, He was referring to every believer. We can only realise this in our own experience when we are prepared to step out and put it to the test. This is not daring to do reckless things just for the sake of being reckless, there is no virtue in that. What I am talking about is daring to act upon God's word.

God is looking for people in these days who will break out of the mould of their small-mindedness and start to believe Him for bigger and greater things. People who take God's word seriously and expect it to work!

Maybe you consider yourselves to be a person of faith. Perhaps you are saying, *"Well I believe and act upon the promises of God."* However, when we bring our lives to the searchlight of His word then sometimes we see a different picture. For example, in John 15 there is another extraordinary statement which promises a life of unlimited potential. If we truly believed it, and acted upon it, then our lives would never be the same again! It is so amazing that Jesus makes the statement twice. This is because He wants to underline the point He is making and also leave us in no uncertainty about what has been said. First of all, at the end of verse 7 He says, *"Ask whatever you will, and it shall be done for you."* And then also in the last part of verse 16 we read, *"…. whatever you ask the Father in my name He will give it to you."*

Imagine living your life not just with a blank cheque, but a blank cheque book, endorsed by a Billionaire! If that was the case, you would walk with a certain air of confidence. Not arrogance or pride, simply confidence. That's exactly what verses 7 and 16 enable us to do. They present to every Christian an open cheque book, backed up by the God of heaven! We, of course, are not talking about asking for a Rolls Royce, or a mansion etc. The promise needs to be qualified in this sense: when we are determined to fulfil our destiny, disciplining ourselves to make radical decisions, and dealing with everything damaging to faith, it then moves us into a position of blessing where we can expect to receive.

We are not automatically in that position, because of all the previous things we have mentioned that get in the way. We must move in our faith and righteousness to that position of obedience to God's word. Now verse seven of John 15 begins to make more sense. It says, *"If you abide in me, and my words abide in you, ask whatever you will, and it shall be done for you."*

When we abide in Him and His word abides in us, then our desires become the same as His; they become one. This is why we can ask anything and we shall receive, because we are asking according to His will. This is totally different to tagging on the end of our prayers the phrase, *"If it be thy will O God."* Very often this is just a 'back door' phrase that people attach to the end of their prayer, just in case what they've asked for doesn't come to pass. We should have the goal of being in the place where we know what God's will is before we pray it. Then we can also speak God's will into situations and prophesy God's word into circumstances.

This was the reason Jesus was so fruitful and effective in all that He did. He already knew God's will and simply spoke it into areas of need. He said,

"…. the Son can do nothing of His own accord, but only what He sees the Father doing; for whatever He does, that the Son does likewise." (John 5:19).

Before Jesus spoke to any sickness, any demon, or any dead body, He already knew what God's will was. In the same way we can abide in our doubts, fears, frustrations etc. or we can believe that we are **destined for Greatness**; to be like Jesus! We have been called to abide in Christ and let His word abide in us. From that position of relationship with the Lord of all creation, we can speak out what we believe to be His will for each situation we meet. Then as He responds, we will bear *much fruit."*

Chapter 2

The Hindrance Of Ungodly Attitudes

It seemed like just another monthly team meeting as around forty of us gathered for business, following a meal together. Little did I know then, the impact that was about to be made on my life.

A quietness descended on the room as we came to prayer, which was broken by the curious sound of running water. In looking up to see what was happening I noticed that Don, the director and team leader of the work, had gone to the kitchen area and for some reason was filling a bowl. He then took a towel and, before doing anything else, read from his Bible the passage where Jesus washed the disciple's feet. We were accustomed to him doing 'unusual' things so this was no great surprise, we simply thought, *"He's probably going to wash everyone's feet."*

Well, I was partly right, but it wasn't everyone's that he had in mind! Complete with bowl in hand, he started to make his way carefully across the crowded room, and you could sense everyone feeling, *"I hope he's not going to start with me!"* It was for this reason we all kept our heads firmly down, so as not to catch his eye and attract any unwanted attention. At this point I became conscious of people shuffling to one side all around me, making space as he came forward. Then I suddenly realised, he was heading towards me! In the stunned silence of the room, this giant of a man, (all 6ft 5 inches) knelt in front of me and said, *"Yan, I know that I've offended you and our relationship is not right. Will you please forgive me and let me wash your feet?"*

You can imagine how humbled I felt at that moment. For months my attitude had not been right towards him. We had disagreed over a number of things quite strongly and I was convinced he was in the wrong! In that incredible moment though, none of that mattered. I knew the wrong was mine because of my attitude.

In stooping down as he did, not just physically, but emotionally, all the pride and resentment that I was harbouring only convicted me more. As he carefully washed and dried my feet, the tension and ill feeling which had existed between us was broken, and we embraced tearfully, being reconciled together.

Our attitudes have a tremendously powerful influence on every part of our life. When these are ungodly in any way, they not only spoil our relationship with others, but can also disrupt us emotionally, afflict us physically and bind us spiritually. Unless we maintain righteousness in this area we will always be limited in what we could be for God. It is possible to achieve a measure of greatness in the eyes of some, but whatever the achievement or success may be, a person's potential will be restricted, and their reputation undermined, where wrong attitudes are present.

The example of a Jewish believer, well known to most Pentecostal pastors throughout the country, illustrates how wrong attitudes damage our credibility. This man has, for several years, attacked in writing, and in public meetings, things like: 'The Faith Movement,' 'The Toronto Blessing,' 'The Pensacola Revival' and the integrity of many leading ministers; denouncing them by name. A few of his comments may well be correct, and I would have to agree with some of his conclusions. However, these remarks are made in such a legalistic, venomous way, that the bitter, proud and judgmental spirit is unmistakable, and his ungodly attitude discredits his argument.

This is why the Bible says,

> *"If I speak in the tongues of men and angels, but have not love, I am a noisy gong or a clanging cymbal. And if I have prophetic powers, and understand all mysteries and all knowledge, and if I have all faith, so as to remove mountains, but have not love, I am nothing. If I give away all I have, and if I deliver my body to be burned, but have not love, I gain nothing."* (1 Corinthians 13:1-3).

All our amazing potential will amount to very little if we are not filled, motivated and controlled by God's love. This is the one quality more than anything else that causes others to see Jesus in us. The absence of this is soon revealed in ungodly attitudes and even though we might feel we've accomplished great things, or are doing mighty works, in reality what we have done becomes meaningless.

As Paul goes on to describe what love is, we see a beautiful picture of Christ; a nature that has an irresistible dynamic about it, attracting the interest and winning the hearts of others. He says,
> *"Love is patient and kind; love is not jealous or boastful; it is not arrogant or rude, love does not insist on its own way; it is not irritable or resentful; it does not rejoice at wrong, but rejoices in the right. Love bears all things, believes all things, hopes all things, endures all things."* (Verse s 4-7).

It is the opposite of each of these characteristics mentioned that express ungodly attitudes and they mar the image of Jesus in us. Every time this is the case, we fall short of our high calling to have a, *"manner of life that is worthy of the Gospel."* (Philippians 1:27).

WHAT ATTITUDES ARE

Our attitudes are more than just opinions on a specific issue or particular responses to certain situations. They are a settled way of thinking lying deep down in our personality, resulting in set behaviour. They are the way we feel and react to the things around us; an outlook that affects all that we say, think and do. Attitudes are expressed not just through our words, but also in our very manner, tone of voice and facial expression.

These responses are revealed in a variety of ways throughout the daily situations of life. They are particularly pronounced where there is disapproval, conflict, stress, competition, ambition, disappointment etc. It is in circumstances that put us under pressure, inconvenience us in some way, or challenge our views, that wrong attitudes come bubbling quickly to the surface.

I am sure we can all recall our reaction to instances while driving, when someone carelessly cuts in front of us, or we are frustrated sitting in a long traffic queue and we begin to get irritable. Often a person is transformed into a completely different 'creature' once they are behind the steering wheel of a car!

Being kept waiting at a supermarket check-out by an assistant who is slow on the till is another classic opportunity for unrighteous attitudes to surface. Then there are times when someone phones us and it is inconvenient, or we see them walking down the path to visit and we'd rather not have them call. A false smile and good impression can be put on at the time, but after they've gone the reality of our hearts is exposed by our attitude.

Even something as trivial as the way we play board-games can be quite revealing. It only takes one game of Monopoly with the best of people to expose the depth of their spirituality! Again in the area of sport when decisions are against us and we feel cheated, or wronged in some way, then sparks can begin to fly!

HOW ATTITUDES ARE FORMED

We were not born with ungodly attitudes, but we were born with a sinful nature, and it is from our flawed character that wrong attitudes begin to develop. This nature that we begin life with, is shaped by a number of major contributing factors, which are a mixture of positive and negative influences. These are:-

(A) *Our Upbringing*

The attitudes, opinions, moral standards and general philosophy of our parents have a significant impact upon our lives as children. The way they communicated and related to each other, handled disputes, and coped with their problems is subconsciously picked up by ourselves when we are young. How we were treated by them in terms of affection, discipline, and general training in how to react to others, influences our attitudes in later life. Also, it is quite common for people, as adults, to find themselves reacting in a certain way and then to recall that what they've said, or the way in which they have said it, was just how one of their parents used to react.

(B) *Life's Painful Experiences*

The 'emotional baggage' we live with from our past brings a fragmentation to our personality which inevitably influences our attitudes and hinders us in reaching the full potential we are capable of. The way we express our opinions, or trust and relate to others, and the belief we have in ourselves to face challenges and grasp new opportunities is damaged where there have been painful experiences.

For some it could be the constant barrage of negative, discouraging and hurtful words they've received over many years. In other cases it might be the pain of a traumatic event like abuse, rejection, personal failure, betrayal by someone, or humiliation, etc.

The type of attitudes that can develop and become part of our personality because of past hurts are: stubbornness, cynicism, aggressiveness, independence, pessimism, anger, rebellion, impatience, selfishness, defensiveness, sarcasm, defeatism, negativity etc.

Some people tend to be extremely over-sensitive and easily upset. Their 'prickly' nature becomes well known and, because they are difficult to get along with, they tend to be quite lonely. Others can be harsh in the way they relate to people and cutting in the things they say. Some are nervously anxious about the approval of others and their constant striving for acceptance makes them over-eager to please.

(C) *Cultural Environment*

Living in an ungodly society that has little time in its values for any thought of submission to Jesus Christ or the God of the Bible, greatly influences people's attitudes. The cultural environment in which most of our time is spent ultimately shapes our thinking. This is evident in the difference between those who come from the 'big city' and those from a small rural village, in their attitudes towards things like friendliness, hospitality and their community in general. In a similar way, the much talked about 'North/South divide' in our nation, and the degree of material wealth that people have, tends to affect their attitudes.

Also, there can be no doubt about the tremendous pressure there is today, particularly on young people, from their peers to conform to the trend of the status quo. When attitudes towards things like fashion, pleasure, sex, success, authority etc. are fed to them by television soaps, films, magazines and the advertising world, then it is no wonder that people's attitudes are so different to that of Christ. This is why the Bible says, *"Do not be conformed to the world but be transformed by the renewal of your mind...."* (Romans 12:2).

(D) *The Word of God*
We read in the scriptures *"Let the word of God dwell in you richly...."* (Colossians 3:16). God's word plays a vital role in shaping our attitudes. However, I have placed this last after the influence of our sin-nature, upbringing, life's painful experiences and cultural environment because we are usually affected by all those other factors first, before God's word has an opportunity to impact our life. It is for this reason Jesus taught that we must be, *"born again."* (John 3:3).

We need to start again with a new nature. Paul, in Ephesians 4:22-24 also refers to the need of, *"putting off"* our old nature and *"putting on"* a new one, *"created after the likeness of God...."* When we are converted we receive a new nature and it is from this that godly attitudes are developed. Basically then, all ungodly attitudes come out of a **'Self-centredness'** and all godly attitudes come out of a **'Christ-centredness.'**

RIGHTEOUS ATTITUDES
Our attitudes are worked out in relationships. It is here that they are developed and shaped in our lives. The key to getting these right is to look at how we relate on a vertical and horizontal level against the commandment Jesus gave when He said,
> *"Thou shalt love the Lord thy God with all thy heart, and with all thy soul, and with all thy mind. This is the first and great commandment. And the second is like unto it, Thou shalt love thy neighbour as thyself."*
>
> (Matthew 22:37-39, AV).

The love of God is the power and spiritual force that influences our entire life, producing righteous attitudes.

Firstly, THE VERTICAL LEVEL

Our relationship with God is the basis from which everything else flows. When this is right, it affects every other area. The reality of our love for God is seen in the following ways:

(A) *Our Attitude Towards Sin*

When we have not got a reverence for God's holiness and a loving respect for His standard of purity our relationship begins to break down. It is then that we become open to all manner of evil influences that disrupt our attitudes and reactions. The example we find in Jesus as to how He felt towards sin is seen in the fact that it was said of Him, *"You love righteousness and hate wickedness."* (Psalm 45:7).

(B) *Willing and Glad Obedience*

Rather than the attitude of reluctance, half-heartedness, or apathy in doing God's will, we are instructed by David to, *"Serve the Lord with gladness!"* (Psalm 100:2). There needs to be a joyful willingness to do what His word says, in whatever we are told to do. Jesus spoke of the way this reveals the genuineness of our love when He said, *"If you love me, you will keep my commandments."* (John 14:15).

(C) *Humble Dependence*

Relying on His strength and ability instead of struggling on in our own power and resources, expresses our love for Him. Jesus said,
".... apart from me you can do nothing."   (John 15:5).
When we hear this, our response should be to take His word seriously and depend entirely on Him, rather than let the attitude of pride and independence express that we can manage alright by ourselves. God through the prophet Zechariah also said,
"..... Not by might, nor by power, but by my Spirit says the Lord of hosts."   (Zechariah 4:6).

(D) *Simple Trust*

When there is trouble around us we express our love for God by not doubting His faithfulness. Instead we have a childlike trust that He is for us and will deliver us. It is very often in the presence of trials that wrong attitudes come out. An example of how we should react is seen in the life of Job. Even when everything was going wrong for him he maintained a right attitude. The Bible says that he,

> "*.... fell upon the ground, and worshiped. And he said, 'Naked I came from my mother's womb, and naked shall I return; the Lord gave, and the Lord has taken away; blessed be the name of the Lord.' In all this Job did not sin or charge God with wrong.*"   (Job 1:20-22).

Rather than having the attitude of grumbling, being negative, feeling sorry for himself and blaming God, he reacted righteously. The sincerity of his love for God was seen in that he didn't backslide as some people do when their prayers aren't immediately answered, or things aren't going well for them. Job's expression of simple trust was that he worshipped and gave thanks.

Secondly, THE HORIZONTAL LEVEL

The importance of our relationship with other people cannot be over emphasised. Once the first part of Jesus' command, to love God with all our being, is established in our lives, then the second half to, "*love your neighbour as you love yourself*" becomes so much easier. The Bible makes it very clear that if we don't have a right attitude towards others, loving unconditionally even those who are difficult to love, then we haven't got a right attitude towards God.

We need to demonstrate the reality of our love for God in practical terms to those around us, particularly in the areas of:-

(A) The Church

The Bible spells out how we are to love one another in the Church; in fact the New Testament is full of teaching on this, for example it says we are to:

Honour One Another

Here is one area in which we are instructed to excel. Paul says, *".... out-do one another in showing honour."* (Romans 12:10). This is such a contrast to the attitudes of criticism, gossiping, belittling, and sarcasm that we find, not only outside the Church, but also frequently within the family of God. Putting other people before ourselves and showing an attitude of honouring those that are around us is always God's way. We ought to esteem all who are in the body of Christ for who they are as a child of God, whether it's the pastor or the janitor of the church. This should also be so, even though we might not always agree with others about how we interpret certain aspects of scripture.

Encourage One Another

A lot of people today are concerned about what they can receive and how they can be blessed, but the attitude of wanting to give and be a blessing seems strangely absent. Regretfully, the attitude of being self-centred and preoccupied with our own needs, always expecting to be ministered to, appears to be more evident amongst Christians. Hebrews 3:13 however says, we are to *"Encourage one another daily, as long as it is called Today."* (NIV).

Serve One Another

One of the ways in which we can encourage others is to have an attitude of willingness about serving them. In Galatians 5:13 we read,
> *".... do not use your freedom as an opportunity for the flesh, but through love be servants of one another."*

If we have a heart to serve others we can be such a blessing in bearing the burden, especially of other workers. All too often in the Church it is the same small few that do the majority of the work. When we recognise though that we all have an important role to play in the body, and we have the desire to serve, then we release the life and blessing of God to flow upon the congregation.

Submit To One Another

This is an attitude that comes right against the spirit of this age where a sense of personal accountability is laughed at, and where all authority is rejected. In Ephesians 5:21 Paul says, *"Be subject to one another out of reverence for Christ."*

The true measure of our reverence for the Lord and His word is seen in how we apply this principle in our relationships. This means there is no place for an attitude of independence, or of being proud and superior. We need to listen to what others have to say, rather than just push forward our ideas. The un-teachable spirit that won't receive admonishment and correction in any way, always expresses an ungodly and destructive attitude.

Forgive One Another

A whole range of ungodly attitudes are prevented from developing and spreading through forgiveness. Things like resentment, bitterness, grudges and ultimately division all begin because of not forgiving those who have hurt or offended us. Ungodly attitudes here not only affect the individuals concerned but also rob the church of God's blessing and power. This is why the Bible says,

> *"Let all bitterness and wrath and anger and clamour and slander be put away from you, with all malice and be kind to one another, tenderhearted, forgiving one another, as God in Christ forgave you."*   (Ephesians 4:31&32).

(B) THE FAMILY

What we hear from God on Sundays has got to be worked out in a real and relevant way within family life throughout the week. This ensures that we are not one thing in the church and something else quite different at home. The family is the smallest working unit of the Church and if the family is not right then the Church will not be right either.

It is often here in family life that negative and destructive attitudes begin to surface. This can be so between husband and wife, children and parents, brothers and sisters, and between in-laws, etc. It is attitudes like selfishness, stubbornness, resentment, moodiness, pride, rebellion, and independence that frequently come out within the family.

Family life today is under major attack because of the liberal views of some, both inside and outside the Church. The break-up of the family is taking place through things like: infidelity, quick divorce, extreme feminist ideas, the confusion of roles, pressure from minority groups such as the 'Gay Movement;' and not least, the television, which has replaced communication in the home with so much that is anti-God in its values.

God's divine order for family life is found in Ephesians chapter five. While the teaching here is clear, it can only work when there is an understanding and commitment to righteous attitudes. Only this will keep the family together and enable it to have a strong effective testimony. Here in verse 22 it says, *"Wives, be subject to your husbands, as to the Lord."*

This speaks of an attitude of submission with a glad and willing respect for the leadership of the man, not being dominated by the husband and responding with a grudging reluctance. It is an attitude of heart that recognises God's divine order and a willingness to live by His instruction.

To the husbands Paul writes, *"Husbands, love your wives, as Christ loved the church and gave Himself for her."* (Ephesians 5:25). When the husband has this attitude of sacrificial commitment towards his wife, putting her needs first in all things, then it makes it easy for the wife to submit and feel secure. The husband's attitude is not one of wanting to dictate and control, rather he is laying down his life for his wife to see her set free to fulfil her full potential. In times of conflict he is reaching out, taking the initiative to bring reconciliation; not waiting for the wife to apologise before harmony is restored. It is then, in this context of mutual respect and commitment, that we see a wonderful sense of unity come into the relationship.

From out of this relationship of loving submission, and sacrificial commitment, it becomes the seed bed for everything that develops within the family home. Into this environment of righteous attitudes children are born, who grow up in the security of how mum and dad relate, and so are influenced by that example.

God's word goes on then to say, *"Children, obey your parents in the Lord for this is right."* (Ephesians 6:1).

Sadly, as our society is today, children seldom have the example of righteous attitudes to grow up with and to model their life upon. It is because of this that they very quickly learn to disrespect what they see in their parents and, in turn, have an attitude of disdain towards all authority. The role model that they are looking at in the home inevitably shapes and makes their own personal attitudes towards others. Out of this lack of respect there comes disobedience and ultimately rebellion.

(C) IN THE WORK PLACE

All too often at work we find attitudes of disinterest, disrespect, disloyalty and discontent, yet it is here, that our responsibility to have a manner of life that commends the gospel is so important. We have, in this situation, a tremendous opportunity to stand out and be a witness to the life-changing power of Christ.

God's instruction for our attitudes in the workplace are found in the words of Paul when he says,

"Be obedient to those who are your masters, with fear and trembling, in singleness of heart, as to Christ; not in the way of eye-service, as men-pleasers, but as servants of Christ, doing the will of God from the heart, rendering service with a good will as to the Lord and not to men, knowing that whatever good any one does, he will receive the same again from the Lord, whether he is a slave or free."

(Ephesians 6:5-8).

"Respect" for our employers is the first thing mentioned here by Paul, rather than making fun of them behind their backs, criticising them and giving them nicknames. If we are not careful we can easily find ourselves drawn into the negative attitudes of others, and in doing so ruin our testimony. God's command in verse 5 says, *"Be obedient with fear and trembling."* Sometimes we might be tempted to feel that certain attitudes can be justified, because of the way we have been treated by our employers. However, in Peter's epistle we are taught that we are to respect and show honour towards our employers, whether they are considered to be good or bad. Peter says,

"Be submissive to your masters with all respect, not only
to the kind and gentle but also to the overbearing."

(1 Peter 2:18&19).

"Loyalty" is the next godly attitude and quality of character that needs to be seen in the work place. This by many today is considered to be 'old fashioned,' and is scoffed at. It is, though, a characteristic that will enable us to stand out as different from others and certainly bring God's blessing of success upon our future.

The attitude of only working hard when we're being watched, or doing as little as we can get away with for as much pay as we can get, is very much in the heart of some. Most employers, though, quickly pick this up and the pretence is soon exposed. In addressing this problem, God's word says we are to work with,

".... singleness of heart, as to Christ; not in the way of
eye-service, as men-pleasers, but as servants of Christ...."

(Ephesians 6:5&6).

Being diligent to do more than the minimum to get by, means we can be trusted to wholeheartedly give our best at all times.

"Contentment" is one other attitude rarely seen in the work place. It is common today to find grumbling, complaining and protesting over the smallest things. Paul's teaching though, is that we are to be,

".... doing the will of God from the heart, rendering
service with a good will...." (Ephesians 6:6&7).

There should be a gladness about what we do and a sincerity as we work that can only come out of being content. To be a cheerful, willing employee in all tasks we are given is an impressive testimony to anyone.

The key to right attitudes in the workplace is to recognise who we are actually working for. This is why verse 5 of Ephesians 6 says our obedience is, *".... as unto Christ,"* also in verse 6, *".... as servants of Christ, doing the will of God from the heart."* And in verse 7, *"rendering service to the Lord and not to men."*

When we see that we are working for God and have been appointed by Him to where we are, not just to earn wages, but to represent Christ, then this gives us a whole new perspective on what we are doing.

HOW WE CHANGE OUR ATTITUDES

For real change to come into our hearts we must recognise God's word as the 'plumb line' for our lives; the standard by which we judge everything else; the final and absolute authority about how we should live. Then *we* must be willing to change so that we are not saying, *"Lord, change my circumstances"* or, *"change those difficult people that I can't get on with,"* but we say, *"Lord, change me!"*

In Philippians chapter two there is a helpful path for us to take if we really want to change in this area. Here we find five positive steps:

Firstly, *Repent* of all wrong motives that have put self first:
    "Do nothing from selfishness or conceit." (verse 3a).
We need to be honest, especially where there has been a hidden agenda of concern about how our action can best work to our advantage. In everything we do, we must take time to be sure that Jesus is Lord of all our life, especially the area of our motivation.

Secondly, *Recognise* the value and significance of other people and seek to encourage their worth. We need to humble ourselves and deal with all pride that suggests we are more important and our opinions are always right. It is by dying to self that we begin to see life from other people's perspective:

"…. in humility count others better than yourselves."

(verse 3b).

Thirdly, *Realise* that others have needs which are equally as pressing as our own. In seeking to be outward looking we must shift the focus of our attention away from our own interests and redirect it towards others. In doing so we are taking time to show concern about their feelings and what is going on in their lives:

"Look not only to your own interests but also to the interests of others." (verse 4).

Fourthly, *Renew* the way we think. Our life is transformed by the renewing of our minds, therefore the example of Christ needs to influence us in every area so that we stop and consider how Jesus would react in each situation we face:

"Your attitude should be the same as that of Christ Jesus …."

(verse 5, NIV).

Fifthly, *Rejoice* even when things aren't going our way. It is by maintaining a spirit of appreciation and gratitude towards God and others that we'll begin to find there's no room for anything but praise!

"Do everything without complaining or arguing …."

(verse 14, NIV).

Chapter 3

The Searching Questions Of God

The amusing story is told of three Pastors who, on their day off, were out playing golf together. They had agreed that the time would enable them to get to know each other on a deeper level and help strengthen their relationships. Having set this goal they committed themselves to be open and honest and for there to be no question that one could not ask of the other.

On arriving back at the changing rooms they began to talk about the personal struggles each had been experiencing. The first pastor, in response to the gentle but professional probing of the others, confessed to having a problem with alcohol and admitted to being a 'secret drinker.' He shared that for years this battle had been going on and it was becoming a great burden to him. The second pastor also responded to the question about how his own life was. He confessed to being addicted to pornography and spoke of how he found it really hard to control his thought life. In both cases understanding and support was expressed by those listening.

The third pastor, who had been full of questions about the struggles his friends had shared, was now strangely quiet. Because of this the other two asked, *"Well, haven't you got anything you want to confess?"*

After an awkward silence the third man replied, *"Well yes, I have actually, ... I'm a compulsive gossiper and I can't wait to get out of this place!"*

At times we can feel certain things are best unsaid because we are not confident that the person we would like to share with can be trusted. Occasionally, questions we'd like to ask are left unspoken because we are not sure that our motives will be seen as genuine. God though, unlike some people, has a sincere concern for each of the struggles we face in life and a deep commitment to helping us move beyond whatever we might be battling with. One of the remarkable ways He accomplishes this is by releasing His saving grace through simple questions. By these He speaks to the root of our problems and brings change in us.

The first thing we must understand before we can grasp this revelation, is that God sees every situation and knows every detail of what is going on in people's lives. This was the truth King David reminded his son Solomon of when he said,
".... the Lord searches all hearts, and understands every plan and thought." (1 Chronicles 28:9).
This same fact was also brought out by the disciple John. Referring to Jesus he said,
".... He knew all men and needed no one to bear witness of man; for He Himself knew what was in man." (John 2:25).

The Lord is also a God of purpose and never does anything without a reason. The puzzling thing is though, throughout scripture we find Almighty God, who has all knowledge, asking questions of others that He already knows the answer to.

Strange as it might appear there is a purpose, and an example of this is found in John 6:1-14 in the account of where five thousand people were miraculously fed. Here Jesus asks Philip, *"How are we to buy bread, so that these people may eat?"* (verse 5b). Then in verse 6 we find the purpose clearly stated: *"This He said to test him, for He Himself knew what He would do."*

We see that in this situation the question came to: (**a**) Draw attention to the problem; (**b**) Direct people's focus towards Himself; (**c**) Demonstrate His miraculous power; and (**d**) Develop the faith of His disciples.

What we learn from this is that the questions which come to us from the Lord are always for our good, and they bring God's help in a variety of ways. For example to unlock situations in our life; bring release; help us see ourselves as He sees us; get out of us what is going on inside; enable us to express our hurts and frustrations; and for our faith to be developed, so that our potential can be maximised.

This is such a contrast to the whispering questions of Satan. He speaks only to destroy God's plan for our life; to restrict us and hold us back from being the person God has purposed us to be. He comes against every child of God to: (a) Attack, (b) Accuse, and (c) Actively undermine their confidence. The motive behind his questions is always evil, just as it was right back in the garden of Eden when man first walked with God. His strategy was clear then and hasn't changed today.

The first thing that Satan does is to ask the question, *" ... ... Did God say, 'You shall not eat of any tree of the garden?'"* (Genesis 3:1b). Immediately doubt is sown into Eve, and he undermines her confidence in what God had already clearly spoken.

The questioning of the enemy is something we can hear throughout our lives as he whispers things like, *"Did God really mean what you thought He said?"-"Does it still apply today?"-"Why did God allow that to happen?"-"Is God really going to use your life?"*

These questions come against us to: (a) Sow doubt, (b) Steal our peace, and (c) Separate us from God.

As we consider God's wisdom, rather than anything the devil has to say to us, let us keep in mind that His questions have a specific purpose. They bring the Lord's grace into our lives by:

Firstly, RELEASING US FROM SIN AND GUILT

One of the most consistent themes of teaching that can be heard today is how God is preparing a people in these end times through whom He can demonstrate His power. We will never fully achieve what God intends us to, whilst there is compromise and unconfessed sin in our lives.

It is for this reason the Bible says,
"For the time has come for Judgement to begin with the household of God...." (1 Peter 4:17).

Any area of unrighteousness in the lives of those in the Church will ultimately be brought out into the light and exposed.

It never ceases to amaze me what some Christians think they can get away with. I was reminded of this on an occasion whilst ministering at a Pentecostal Church in the south. The meeting was going well and everyone in the congregation was enthusiastically entering into the worship. Four people particularly stood out to me as, with hands raised, their enthusiasm was unrestrained. Towards the end of the meeting there came a tremendous awareness of God's presence and the Holy Spirit moved in a powerful way, bringing conviction.

Among those who came forward for prayer were the four people who had caught my eye earlier; a husband and wife and a young man with his girlfriend. They were wanting to repent of their sin and be set free from the bondage they had come into. Each confessed to watching pornographic videos together and of being in a 'four in a bed' situation with each other.

However foolish our disobedience might be, God doesn't deal with our sin by coming with a big stick of condemnation to beat us. Rather, one of the ways He brings conviction is through questions to our conscience. These confront us with the challenge of His standard and draw us out into the light of reality. An example of this is found in Genesis 3. The searching question asked here by the Lord is simply, *"Where are you Adam?"* (verse 9).

It seems a strange thing for God to say because He obviously knew where to locate Adam, but what was being asked wasn't for His own benefit, it was to help Adam see the consequences of his disobedience.

Adam had sinned. He had disobeyed God, and the direct result was that fear came into him, so he hid from the Lord. It is interesting to notice also that he not only hides from God, but from his wife as well, and she from him. They both cover up their nakedness and are ashamed. The same effect of sin and guilt is found today. We hide from God and also cover up and hide who we are and where we're really at, from one another.

The question gently asked by God, *"Adam where are you?"* comes therefore to draw him out of hiding; out from the shadows and into the light. It helped Adam face up to where he was in his relationship with God and how he had got there. He was brought to the place where he had to acknowledge the reality that his relationship was broken, and he could no longer stand confidently before the Lord.

This same question is something that will be heard in our own hearts if there is unconfessed sin in our life. We might hear it as we are trying to enter into praise and worship, whilst taking Communion, during the preaching, or throughout the daily circumstances of life-especially when we feel under pressure. At such times God speaks to our conscience, simply asking, *"Where are you in your relationship with me?"* We regularly need to face that question and re-evaluate where we are, so that we make sure we're not covering up anything from the Lord, or wearing masks of pretence with one another.

It is as we respond in confession to what we hear God asking that we find forgiveness, release from all guilt, and restoration in our relationship with the Lord. Even when we feel crushed by condemnation and attacked by the accusing finger of others, the Lord speaks to set us free.

This is what happened with the woman who was caught in the act of adultery. Everyone was condemning her and the religious leaders were wanting to stone her to death. They came to Jesus, challenging Him with their questions. Trying to catch Him out they asked:
>*"In the law Moses commanded us to stone such. What do you say about her?"*   (John 8:5).

The reply from the Lord to this was,
>*"Let him who is without sin among you be the first to throw a stone at her."*   (verse 7b).

The account then tells us that, from the eldest to the youngest, silently they all left, until she was standing there alone with Jesus, the only one who could condemn her. Jesus then asks,
>*".... Woman, where are they? Has no one condemned you?"*   (verse 10).

Jesus knew the answer; He was aware of why they had gone, but what He was asking was for the purpose of meeting the woman's need. He wanted her to see that no one had any right to condemn her, for they also were sinners. The question was brought so that release from guilt and cleansing from the sin could be found. This same liberating truth was proclaimed by Paul when he asked,

*"Who shall bring any charge against God's elect? It is
God who justifies; who is it to condemn?"* (Romans 8:33&34).

No one has any right to condemn us when we come, in confession, out of sin and are committed to stay in Christ Jesus.

Secondly, HEALING OUR EMOTIONAL PAIN

All of us have experienced emotional pain of some kind or another. We can be easily hurt and damaged by the attitudes, words and actions of others. Events that go back many years, that we've suppressed, can cause us to have bottled up emotions.

We can have wounded spirits in need of God's healing power because of disappointment and discouragement. Circumstances that have taken us by surprise can leave us emotionally dazed and confused, feeling no-one really understands. At times we can feel completely alone and in a position where we don't know why things have happened in the way that they have.

Not long ago, at a meeting in Lancashire, I recall a lady coming out for prayer. She was emotionally devastated and unable to make any sense of her situation. She shared that her husband had left her and their five children and was flying abroad to set up home with a woman he'd contacted on the Internet. Although he had never met this person before, he was prepared to give up everything for her. What was happening just seemed beyond understanding and was causing considerable distress to the whole family.

Regardless of what pain we've experienced, the Bible says,

*"The Lord is near to the broken-hearted, and saves the
crushed in spirit."* (Psalm 34:18).

One of the ways that He draws near and ministers His healing power is to speak to us gently with a question. A good example of this is found in the account of Mary at the tomb of Jesus. She had come to pay her last respects, but as she arrives there, all that she can find are the grave-clothes. Thinking that someone had stolen the body of Jesus she is broken-hearted, confused and in an emotional turmoil. Many thoughts rush through her mind as she stands there alone, sobbing. The Lord then speaks to her with this strange question:

"…. Woman, why are you weeping? Whom do you seek?"

(John 20:15).

Jesus, of course, knew why she was so distressed and who she was looking for, but the question comes for a reason; to bring the nearness of the Lord's presence to her and reassure her that there was someone who cared about her situation. Jesus then goes on to reveal Himself personally as he speaks her name, saying, "Mary" (verse 16). That personal, individual call transformed her mourning into dancing. All her sadness was changed into joy when she realised it was the Lord!

With the different circumstances that we go through, and the various emotions we feel, the Lord also gently comes alongside us with a similar question, - "Why are you weeping?" - " What is making you sad and discouraged?" - " What has upset you?"

He already knows the answer and is not asking for His own interest. The question is to remind us that He is alive and closer to us than we could ever imagine! Jesus wants us to know that He does care about what we are going through and is willing to be involved in whatever we may be struggling with.

As we hear Him speaking to our own hearts asking, "What is it you are looking for?" we are reminded that in turning to Him, all we are searching for will be found. Also, in giving us the opportunity to express how we feel, it helps us to let out all that has been bottled up inside ourselves.

Thirdly, RESTORING US FROM A FEELING OF FAILURE

When we feel that we've let the Lord down in some way, or we've not lived up to our own aspirations and other people's expectations, it is then that a crushing sense of failure overtakes us. Sometimes when we've wanted to do so much and have declared that our lives were going to accomplish great things for the Lord, we find that the reality is very different.

No matter how many times we may have failed in the past, we should never let this determine our future. For example: twice the American General, Douglas MacArthur was refused admission to Westpoint, but the third time he was accepted and marched into the history books. The English writer and Nobel laureate, Rudyard Kipling, received a rejection letter from the San Francisco Examiner saying, *"Sorry Mr Kipling, but you just don't know how to use the English language"*.

After a lifetime of defeats, at 62 years Winston Churchill became one of Britain's greatest Prime Ministers. American inventor Thomas Edison tried over 2,000 experiments before bringing to the world the electric light bulb. A reporter asked how it felt to fail so often. He replied, *"I never failed once; it just happened to be a 2,000 step process!"*

The frustration of failure can be felt by ourselves as Christians because of many things. For instance, failing in our witness to those at work; falling into temptation; weakness in our personal discipline towards our devotional life, and fruitlessness in our ministry etc. It is in these situations of failure that the question from God comes to us just as it did to Peter in John 21:15-17. Here was a man who felt a total failure. Peter had made such a great claim of always standing for Jesus and never letting Him down. However, when the first test came he denied ever knowing Jesus with oaths and curses.

Peter, full of regret and overwhelmed by shame for what he had done, meets the Lord after the resurrection. Jesus draws alongside him and begins to address his feeling of failure and worthlessness by asking the simple question, *"Simon, son of John, do you love me?...."* (verse 15).

Again, of course, Jesus knew the answer to that. He knew Peter's heart, but there was a work of sovereign grace taking place here. Three times Peter had denied Jesus and three times he was being asked, *"Do you love me?"* Then following each of these questions Jesus gave him the instructions, *"Feed my lambs."-"Tend my sheep."-"Feed my sheep."*

Peter must have felt useless because of his failure; his life no longer seemed to have any purpose. Jesus, though, was reminding him of the three times he had failed, and three times was saying in effect, *"I've got a ministry for you to fulfil and I know you will complete it, because you love me."*

Through this questioning the Lord was restoring Peter to the place where he could see that Jesus was prepared to trust him again.

We all need reminding that Jesus is the God of the second chance! When we have failed and not done what we intended, the Lord doesn't wash his hands of us, rather in compassion and love He restores us. The one question beyond anything else that needs to be brought into focus is, *"My son, my daughter, do you love me?"* It comes to remind us that the most important thing to the Lord is not our **Performance** but our **Passion** of love for Him.

What was being asked helped Peter reaffirm his desire to live and work for the Lord. Because of the genuine love Peter had, he was able to move on and complete the task Jesus eventually gave him. Also, later on in his ministry he encouraged others from what he'd personally been through. This one-time failure was able to say with strong conviction,

> *"After you have suffered a little while, the God of all grace, who has called you to His eternal glory in Christ, will Himself restore, establish, and strengthen you."*
>
> (1 Peter 5:10).

Fourthly,
CONQUERING OUR SHYNESS AND SELF-CONSCIOUSNESS

Very often people today are restricted and held back by their self-consciousness. There is a natural shyness we have about sharing our faith and speaking up for Christ as opportunities are given. The same is true about praying publicly or stepping out in the gifts of the Holy Spirit; we can be uneasy about moving on in this way and so are held back from being all we could be.

Just this last week while preaching at a Baptist Church in Leicester, someone responded for prayer with this particular problem. She was an attractive woman who had a brightness and confidence in her face when she spoke to anyone on a one-to-one level, but she knew her life was restricted. Even though her love for the Lord was obvious she said, *"I'm so nervous about speaking out publicly and feel afraid to express myself in the meetings; will you ask the Lord to set me free?"*

As we prayed together for that release, the power of God came upon her and she immediately began to lift up her voice in praise, at the front of the church, before all the congregation!

The Lord asks a question in Mark chapter five that helps a woman who had come for physical healing to move beyond her self-consciousness and shyness. She had spent much on doctors but her condition was only getting worse. Because of this she wanted to come to Christ and receive a miracle. She didn't want to cause any fuss or draw attention to herself, all she wanted was to touch Jesus, be healed and go on her way quietly. There are many such people today who would prefer to be 'secret believers;' those who turn to God for their needs to be met, but are reluctant to publicly stand for Christ.

One question was asked by Jesus, however, that changed this woman's life. While excited crowds were pressing upon Him, He says, *".... Who touched my garments?"* (verse 30b). Jesus knew exactly who it was, even though there were so many around Him, but He wanted to draw the woman out to where she was visible. Other people could then hear her testimony of what God had done, and see for themselves the evidence of His power. The question draws an open confession of faith, giving an opportunity for someone who had received God's help to speak out and share it with others.

A similar question comes to us when we have known God's help and yet have not wanted to testify about it. Jesus would say to us, *"Who has received something from me?"* - *"What prayers have I answered in your life?"*

Jesus, through this woman, wanted to build faith in the lives of those that were in the crowd, and He wants to do the same today. His purpose is, that those with problems and difficulties might hear from us what He's done, and have faith for themselves.

How can we remain silent when we consider the many answers to prayer we've received and all the good things that God has done for us? The Psalmist, David, certainly couldn't, nor should we. His appreciation motivated him to say,

> *"I have told the glad news of deliverance in the great congregation; I have not restrained my lips, as thou knowest, O Lord. I have not hid thy saving help within my heart, I have spoken of thy faithfulness and thy salvation; I have not concealed thy steadfast love and thy faithfulness from the great congregation."* (Psalm 40:9&10).

Fifthly, BUILDING IN US OVERCOMING FAITH
In moving forward we need overcoming faith to press beyond all the problems and barriers that confront us. When our circumstances appear hopeless, and at times it seems as though our situation is never going to change; when we feel we've lived with the difficulty so long that our expectation for it being any different is low, or non-existent, it's then that doubts begin to come in. We are tempted then to rationalise our situation and settle for how things are.

This must have been how Bartimaeus, the blind beggar, felt in Mark 10:46-52. As we picture him in our mind's eye, we see his torn dirty garments, his matted dusty hair, he probably didn't smell too good either! Life amounted to very little for this man. In the eyes of others he was a 'nobody'. He had no purpose for living, no sense of belonging, no feeling of worth, and no hope of his circumstances ever changing. Bartimaeus must have felt lonely, helpless and hopeless. But there came a moment in his life when he was set free from all that bound him. A dull, ordinary day was transformed by a miracle!

As he sensed the bustling crowd and heard the shouts of excitement he heard that Jesus was coming his way. He knew in his heart that this was the moment that was going to change his life. He wasn't going to let the opportunity pass him by, so he lifted up his voice and shouted, *".... Jesus, Son of David, have mercy on me!"* (verse 47). Even though the crowd spun round on him and told him to be silent, still he shouted out all the more. He didn't allow the barrier of people's opinions, or any other obstacle to stop him!

Then Jesus called for him to come, and it's at this point a very puzzling question is asked by Jesus. The one who has all knowledge and sees every situation asks, *"What do you want me to do for you?"* (verse 51a).

Jesus didn't need much discernment regarding his need. This man had been blind from birth; he was obviously blind, anyone could have identified what his need was. Jesus, however, took time to ask the question because He wanted to give an opportunity for this man to release his faith.

The Bible tells us how powerful faith can be when it says, *".... this is the victory that overcomes the world, our faith"* (1 John 5:4).

No matter what problems we have, and regardless of how hard our situation might be, faith is always an 'overcomer'. The question for Bartimaeus, therefore, was to help him be specific and definite about what he was hoping for. Jesus wanted him to confess with his lips what he was saying he believed in his heart.

Notice the beggar hadn't thought, as many think today, *"Jesus knows my situation, so there's no need for me to call out; I'll just leave it to Him."* Nor did he say, as some people say in their praying, *"Lord if it be your will ...* " The response of the one in need and the attitude that brought the breakthrough was specific and clear. He said, *"Master, let me receive my sight."* (verse 51b). He nailed it down and stated plainly his desire!

In our circumstances also, we need to listen to God speaking to us as He says, *"What do you want me to do for you?"* With the situations of sickness, financial struggle, difficult relationships, frustration in ministry, uncertainty about the future, conflict at work etc., our response needs to be concrete, specific and definite as we expect a breakthrough to come. This is crucial, not for God's ears, but for our own heart. We must confess God's word and what we believe He is able to do.

LISTENING FOR GOD'S VOICE

Jesus said, *"He who is of God hears the words of God...."* (John 8:47). We need to be careful not to miss what God is saying, by only expecting to hear Him in dramatic and spectacular ways. It is not just at large meetings, or through 'big names' that God reveals Himself. Very often He speaks in *"a still small voice"*, just as He did with Elijah in 1 Kings 19:12.

Here a great man of faith is broken, depressed and at an end of wanting to live anymore. Into this situation God's presence draws near to him on Mount Horeb, bringing renewal and restoration. This happened not in the breath-taking and sensational ways that Elijah had known throughout his life; it was not in the *"strong wind"*, the *"earthquake"*, or the *"mighty fire"*, that 1 Kings 19 speaks of. God's voice was heard and Elijah's deepest needs were met in the gentle stillness of a *"small voice"*!

As you seek to hear the voice of the Holy Spirit speaking either to your conscience, through your circumstances, in His Word, or through other people etc., the following steps can be helpful:

(A) Start to believe that there is an immense amount of potential still undiscovered and unreleased within you. Paul recognised this in the Christians at Ephesus. He saw that a vital area of their lives had been overlooked and they needed a revelation about this. His earnest prayer for them therefore was,

> *".... Having the eyes of your hearts enlightened, that you may know.... what is the immeasurable greatness of His power in those who believe...."*   (Ephesians 1:18&19).

(B) Take heart that God sees where you are at, and what problems you have. Everything about your life; every detail, and every need is known to Him. There is nothing that affects you that He is not aware of. Mindful of this the Psalmist, David, says,

> *"O Lord, thou hast searched me and known me! Thou knowest when I sit down and when I rise up; thou discernest my thoughts from afar. Thou searchest out my path and my lying down, and art acquainted with all my ways."* (Psalm 139:1-3).

(C) Be alert to what God may say throughout the day, but also commit yourselves to coming aside from life's distractions and pressures, to be alone with Him. Jesus spoke about the importance of this when He taught, *"When you pray, go in to your room and shut the door....."* (Matthew 6:6). Also, in Psalm 46:10 the command we find there is, *"Be still, and know that I am God...."*

(D) Thank God for His faithfulness in not giving up on you and approach Him with a grateful heart. The Bible says,

> *"Enter His gates with thanksgiving, and His courts with praise!"*   (Psalm 100:4a).

Praise Him for the fact that His hand is upon your life and He is committed to finishing the work He has started within you. This was Paul's confidence for the Christians at Philippi when he said,

> *"I am sure that He who begun a good work in you will bring it to completion at the day of Jesus Christ."*
> (Philippians 1:6).

(E) Open yourself completely to the searchlight of His Holy Spirit and simply ask Him to speak to you. Then listen for any area of your life that needs to be surrendered. Perhaps something that you need to confess, or that you are holding back. It might be something He wants you to do, or an area of hurt, fear, doubt, frustration etc. that you need help in. The wise council that Eli gave to Samuel when he was trying to hear God's voice is helpful for ourselves also. His advice was for him to say, *"Speak Lord, for thy servant hears."*   (1 Samuel 3:9).

(F)   Determine before God that whatever He says, you are going to open your heart and let Him bring change.   We must see our responsibility to act upon what we hear and co-operate with the convicting work of the Holy Spirit. The doorway through which God enters our circumstances is more often than not our own hearts. This is why His word says,

> *"Behold, I stand at the door and knock; if anyone hears*
> *my voice and opens the door, I will come in to him...."*
>
> (Revelation 3:20).

It is as we hear His voice, which sometimes comes to us in the form of questions, and we respond, that the Lord will enter into the circumstances of our lives with resurrection power!

Chapter 4

Friendship With God

Some years ago I heard the story of an antique dealer, who was a very shrewd businessman. He would travel throughout the country visiting second-hand shops, trying to find the best possible bargain he could, without paying too much money. One day he was looking around the back street areas of a small town, when he came across a dingy looking second-hand store.

As he went inside to browse through the goods, he noticed, that in the far corner there was a large, fat, black cat drinking milk from an old bowl. He looked with interest, then suddenly realised that what the cat was drinking from was no old bowl, it was a priceless antique! Chuckling to himself he thought, *"The old man in the shop doesn't realise what he's got there; I'll get that old bowl for next to nothing."* So up to the shopkeeper he went.

"Excuse me," the dealer politely said,*" I notice that you have a beautiful black cat over in the corner there, and I've been searching for one just like that for years. Tell me, how much will you take for that lovely cat?"*

The shopkeeper thought for a moment, then said, *"Give me £95 and the cat is yours."*

Without any hesitation the antique dealer reached into his jacket, took out his wallet and quickly paid across the £95, before the shopkeeper could change his mind. Then as he picked up the cat, stroking it gently he said, *"I see that the cat has grown rather attached to that old bowl down there and it's not worth very much; I'll just take it with me as I go on my way home."*

As the antique dealer reached forward to pick up the bowl, the shopkeeper grabbed his arm firmly and said, *"You put that bowl back down there. That's the best 'Cat Seller' I've ever had!"*

Trying to get away with giving the minimum for the most is quite a common attitude in society today, and it has even crept into the Church. People want the blessing of God's power and to live in the richness of His promises, but they are not always willing to pay the full price attached to this. Whilst salvation is a free gift from God, if we are going to get the most out of it, then it will cost us everything! This is especially the case in our relationship with the Lord, and is essential if we are to realise our full potential.

The depth of our relationship speaks volumes to those around us who are looking on and observing our lives. Without us saying a word, there should be something about us that can bring both encouragement and challenge; something that can stir up hope in others, for what they themselves can know.

It was said in the Bible of both Noah and Enoch, that they *"Walked with God."* After they had died this was recorded as a lasting testimony about them, for our instruction. I can't think of any greater accolade to give to someone, nor any finer epitaph to leave behind after death than this. The foundation of all God has called us to is built upon our friendship with Him, and it is this that will speak powerfully to others.

A few years ago, while attending a Christian camp in Lincoln with my wife and family, I was reminded once again about the importance of this friendship and the message it communicates. We are not 'campers' by any stretch of the imagination, in fact it would be true to say that camping is something we carefully avoid. On this occasion though, we thought it would be good for the children, so we happily booked in. As it happened our few days there were particularly wet, cold and windy, but in spite of this it was a time of meeting with God.

What made such a deep impression upon me, and is a lasting memory to this day, wasn't the excellent quality of music led by Chris Bowater, or the eloquent, anointed preaching that included people like

Gerald Coates. Nor was it the efficient, smooth running administration of the camp. The one thing that made an impact on my life was to be amongst people who had a deep love for God and a desire, whatever the cost, to know Him better. The reality and intensity of their walk with the Lord spoke to me and caused me to look at my own relationship. As I reflected on this, the Scripture written by Daniel came to mind, when he said, *".... the people that do know their God, shall be strong, and do exploits."* (Daniel 11:32b, AV).

This verse from Daniel was spoken by a man that knew the cost of walking with God, and he is an example to us of someone who also experienced His mighty power to accomplish an amazing work. As we look more closely at his words let us consider:

Firstly, THE PROSPECT OF FRIENDSHIP WITH GOD

When Daniel states, *"the people that do know their God ...."* who exactly is he referring to? Are they a select few, a spiritual elite, or some special breed of Christian? The answer to this is no. They are the ones who have decided that 'knowing God' is the most important thing in their lives; ordinary individuals who are not satisfied simply with 'meetings,' religious activities, or a mediocre experience.

These people are the ones who want to live 100% for Jesus and they express the same attitude spoken of by Paul when he said,

"Whatever gain I had, I counted as loss for the sake of Christ. Indeed I count everything as loss because of the surpassing worth of knowing Christ Jesus my Lord."

(Philippians 3:7&8).

This all-consuming desire and first passion in Paul's life is again mentioned in verse 10 when he prays, *"That I might know Him and the power of His resurrection."*

Many Christians today want the power, and are chasing exciting 'manifestations,' but few are willing to get to grips with 'knowing' the person. The one thing more than anything else that the Lord always looks for is an attitude of reality in our relationship with Him. God has made it wonderfully possible for each of us to know friendship with Him. This is why we read in Ephesians 2:13,

> "…. *You who once were far off have been brought **near** in the blood of Christ.*"

Again, the same thought is expressed by the writer to the Hebrew Christians when he says, *"Let us draw **near**, in full assurance of faith…."* (Hebrews 10:22).

The intention of the cross was always that we might know a close relationship; not one that is distant and distracted by the things of this world, but a relationship of love. David, spoke of this with an intense desire when he said,

> *"As the deer pants for streams of water, so my soul pants for you, O God. My soul thirsts for God, for the living God."*
> (Psalm 42:1&2, NIV).

The response that the Lord looks for from His people is that every fibre of our being and every breath that is within us is earnestly reaching out in love to Him.

Our love for God is far more important to Him than our service, ministry, office in the Church, Bible knowledge, or the size of our congregation. Ultimately, it is not what we do, but who we are in God that really counts. Our sense of security, significance and self-worth does not rest in what we've achieved; it is not our activity for God that is important, it is our intimacy with Him that really counts. One of the most remarkable examples in the Bible that refers to this level of relationship is found in Exodus 33:11a. Here it says,

> *"Thus the Lord used to speak to Moses face to face, as a man speaks to his friend."*

This phrase, *"face to face"* expresses unrestricted communion in which nothing is hidden or held back. As we think of it in human relationships we are reminded of 'eye ball contact.' When you are talking with this close proximity to someone you begin to see beneath the veneer of a person's life to where they are really at. This is why it's often said that, *"The eyes are the windows of the soul."* The phrase face to face, speaks of a relationship that is transparent, open and honest.

Regretfully, the word *"friend"* seems to have lost its meaning today in the same way that the term 'love' has. For example, we hear it used frequently in the House of Lords and the House of Commons. In the same breath as scathing attacks and sarcastic remarks, politicians will say, *"My honourable friend"* or, *"My noble friend"* and the term really doesn't mean anything.

A true friend, however, is someone you respect and enjoy spending time with. In their company you aren't bored, constantly looking at your watch, hoping they are going soon. Your mind isn't distracted, wandering onto other things as they are talking to you. With a true friend you find yourself able to talk easily and the hours just fly by. You don't feel that you've got to keep the conversation going, or get into a panic when there's a lull in what is being said; you can relax and be yourself.

There is no pretence; no need to wear a mask; you can be natural. You are able to share your joys and sorrows, your victories and struggles. There is a mutual trust and warmth; a confidence that they really do care and are showing a genuine interest. You know that they say what they mean and mean what they say. A true friend also knows all there is to know about you, but still loves you just the same.

The prospect of friendship is something that God holds out to each one of us. This is why the Bible says,
"There are friends who pretend to be friends, but there is
a friend who sticks closer than a brother." (Proverbs 18:24).
God is looking for this sort of relationship again, just as He had with Adam right back at the beginning of creation. For friendship to work though, it has to be two-way. God wants to know friendship with us, but if we are to find friendship with Him we must reach out as well, making known our commitment that whatever the cost, we want to be a friend of God!

Secondly, **THE PROCESS OF FRIENDSHIP WITH GOD**
Here is where the challenge begins to confront us and we find there are no short cuts. As we look at the life and example of Moses we see

that he was led along a path and brought through a process to the place where he could, *"talk with God face to face as a man would speak to a friend."* This same process is common to all people and it is a similar path that we will need to move along if we want to experience the intimacy that he found.

Daniel 11:32 says, *"The people that do **know** their God...."* In God's original design, knowledge of a person was always relational. It implied an intimate, personal relationship. We see this mentioned three times in Genesis 4:

*"Now Adam **knew** Eve his wife, and she conceived and bore Cain."* (verse 1a).

*"Cain **knew** his wife and she conceived and bore Enoch."* (verse 17a).

*"Adam **knew** his wife again, and she bore a son and called his name Seth."* (verse 25a).

This is clearly not referring to an intellectual knowledge of someone. God is using the imagery of when a husband and wife are fully known, in the deepest most intimate sense of that word. This knowledge of God brings new life and fruitfulness into our daily living.

For Moses, friendship with God did not happen right away. There is no such thing as instant intimacy in any meaningful relationship. It takes time, requires sacrifice and demands commitment. There is a process of discovery that needs to take place, and this is what we see happening to Moses.

(A) *God's Salvation*
With Moses, his knowledge of God began in Exodus 2:1-10. It was built on personal experience. The first thing that he knew right from when he was a baby hidden in the bulrushes was God's salvation. He was protected from the edict of Pharaoh who wanted to kill all the first-born children of every Israelite. Moses knew he had been saved from the very sentence of death.

It is here that all personal knowledge of God must begin. However, for a lot of people their experience never moves beyond the knowledge of being 'saved.' It is wonderful to know salvation; we should always be grateful for what Jesus accomplished on the cross in saving us from a lost eternity, but this is just the beginning. For some Christians though, this is where they stop in their experience. They settle down, thankful for the forgiveness of God and assured that they are no longer going to hell, but never seem to move beyond that point.

(B) *A New Dimension Of Thinking*

The next stage along this process for Moses was the personal discovery of the supernatural presence of God in Exodus 3:1-3. Moses here is confronted by the burning bush. He had never before experienced such an extraordinary sight. The bush was enveloped in flames but not consumed. Even more remarkable than this was that the voice of God came from the centre of this bush, speaking to him personally by name. At this stage in the process God was drawing Moses into a new dimension of thinking. His mind had to be raised above the level of logic; beyond the natural realm of human understanding.

There are many today who are stuck at this stage in the process. They miss the blessing of God and the new thing that He wants to do simply because not everything they see or hear fits into the framework of what can be understood with the mind. They want to dot every 'I', cross every 'T' and analyse every situation until they understand it with human reasoning before they will accept it.

God is Spirit; He is supernatural! His word says, *"For my thoughts are not your thoughts, neither are your ways, my ways...."* (Isaiah 55:8). Some people are always trying to bring God down to the level of their minds, attempting to put Him in a box of their own rational thinking and expectation. Their own preconceived ideas restrict what He is able to do for them; they are stuck and unable to really know God as a friend because this whole area of the supernatural is a blind spot to them. It is for this reason the Bible says,

> *"Trust in the Lord with all your heart, and do not rely on your own insight."* (Proverbs 3:5).

(C) *The Holiness of God*

The next discovery Moses makes about God is absolutely fundamental to his experience, and the same is true for us. We will never know Him as a friend without honouring the truth in our lives that God is Holy. This is a place where some, because of compromise, have become stuck in the process, and yet the reality of purity must be firmly established in our hearts.

The first message that came out of the burning bush was,
"Do not come near; put off your shoes, from your feet, for the place on which you are standing is holy ground."

(Exodus 3:5).

God was bringing Moses to the place of communion *"face to face"*, but first had to say, *"do not come near."* He had to put a separation between Himself and Moses so that he would learn a reverence and respect for the righteousness of God.

This fear of the Lord is a characteristic of every revival. In every out-pouring of the Holy Spirit, a sense of awe comes upon people as they are confronted with God's holiness. Isaiah, the prophet, spoke of this when he was referring to a sovereign move of God bringing change to the desert place and the wilderness. In the middle of the chapter, right at the heart of an extraordinary out-pouring of the Spirit he says,
"And a highway shall be there, and it shall be called the Holy Way; the unclean shall not pass over it, and fools shall not err therein."   (Isaiah 35:8).

Isaiah himself was transformed when he *"saw the Lord."* (Isaiah 6:1-5). He was convicted of his sin and hypocrisy as the holiness of God confronted him.

Nobody can move forward in their Christian experience without facing His holiness. How can we know Him as friend when there are things in our life that we hold on to which grieve the Holy Spirit?

The reaction of Moses at this stage is very interesting. It is early days for him in this process, he still has a long way to go and we see this in verse 6 of Exodus 3: *".... Moses hid his face, for he was afraid to look at God."*

(D) *God Is Always Faithful To His Promises*

Moses moves on now to learn that God is a covenant-keeping God and will always be true to His word. It is difficult to know Him as a friend if we doubt this; if we can't trust Him to keep His promises. We must be single-minded in our confidence that He says what He means, means what He says, and will do what He says He will do! The way God accomplishes this in the heart of Moses is seen in the second message that comes out of the burning bush:

"I am the God of your father, the God of Abraham, the God of Isaac and the God of Jacob." (Exodus 3:6a).

This wasn't simply an impressive statement or nice phrase that was being spoken. Throughout the Old Testament these words occur consistently and have great significance. Often when God wanted to underline His promise, reinforce His character, or was about to do something extraordinary, that same phrase was used.

To Abraham, Isaac and Jacob, an identical covenant had been made. This was that from nowhere God would raise up a nation who would be the means of blessing the nations of the world. From nothing He would establish a people who would bear testimony to His greatness, power and faithfulness.

At this particular moment though, as God was dealing with Moses, the Israelites were in bondage in Egypt; they were slaves. There was no way they were going to bless anyone, or bear testimony to God's character. For many years they had been held captive with no possibility of their circumstances changing. God, however, was about to do something; He was going to bring deliverance. Therefore the Lord was saying, in effect, that the promise He had made those many years ago to Abraham, Isaac and Jacob had not been forgotten, it was going to be fulfilled.

The challenging thing about this for us is that whenever God begins to speak about what He intends to do, or we are stirred concerning His promises, invariably He then says, *"...and I want to use you!"* We are at that moment reminded of His call upon our lives and that He has a plan and purpose for us to fulfil. This is the next stage Moses now comes to.

(E) *The Call of God To Service*

Moses discovered that God had a job for him to do, and was able to use ordinary people for extraordinary tasks. As the Lord speaks to him we see that the next message from out of the bush is,

"Come, I will send you to Pharaoh that you may bring forth my people, the sons of Israel, out of Egypt." (verse 10).

The response of Moses to this call is so typical of our own. When God stirs us up to step out in faith, to take on new responsibilities, or to go somewhere that we aren't confident about, we panic and start to look at ourselves. Our focus becomes centred on our weaknesses and inadequacies rather than on His unfailing promises and His unlimited power.

Five times in Exodus chapter 3 & 4 Moses made excuses. He was saying that he didn't want to do the job because he felt inadequate about his personal credibility and, after all, his speech impediment made it impossible anyway.

One of the most interesting things we learn at this stage is that while Moses knew himself, he clearly didn't really know his God. He knew his limitations, weaknesses and frailty, and he allowed those things to overshadow his knowledge of God. If he had really known God, all those other things would have been unimportant.

(F) *The Equipping of God*

The turning point for Moses comes at this next stage in the process. He discovers that God's anointing and authority will be his. This is what brings the breakthrough and starts to build the confidence of Moses. In Exodus 4:2-9 he learns that he doesn't have to go out in his own strength. The task given to him was not to be attempted in his own ability, it was on the supernatural power and miraculous ability of God that he was to depend. This same lesson is something we also need to learn, until we depend entirely on the anointing of God for all we have been called to do.

God establishes this in the heart of Moses in the most remarkable way, and it is another example of what was mentioned in the previous chapter about how God uses questions to impart His grace to us. In Exodus 4:2 the Lord asks,

"What is that in your hand?"

God knew what it was. It was just a rod that he was holding, nothing special in itself, but then God says,

"Cast it on the ground." (verse 3a).

As he does so, it miraculously turns into a snake. Then he is told to pick up the snake by the tail and as he obeys, it turns back into a rod again. God then says,

"Put your hand into your bosom." (verse 6a).

When he does this his hand becomes full of leprosy. God instructs him then to put his hand back into his bosom and miraculously the leprosy is gone.

Following these two amazing miracles God goes on to say,

"If they will not believe those two signs or heed your voice, you shall take some water from the Nile, and pour it on the dry ground; and the water will become blood...."

(verse 9).

As Moses obeys he witnesses the miracle God said would happen.

It isn't difficult to understand what the Lord was doing at this stage in the process. He was strengthening the heart of Moses to see it was through "signs and wonders" his mission would be completed. Release from the bondage of the enemy was going to be brought about by the supernatural power of God and not by the ability of man. All that was required of Moses was his absolute obedience to God's word.

This is what happened to the disciples in the New Testament. God had to teach them this same important truth. He had called them to an incredible task, something that was impossible in their own ability and so He said,

> *"Go into all the world and preach the gospel to the whole creation..... And these signs will accompany those who believe: in my name they cast out demons; they will speak in new tongues; they will pick up serpents, and if they drink any deadly thing, it will not hurt them; they will lay their hands on the sick, and they will recover."* (Mark 16:15-18).

Then in verse 20 we read,

> *"And they went forth and preached everywhere, while the Lord worked with them and confirmed the message by the signs that attended it."*

God is still looking for a people today who will depend on His anointing and obey His directions so that release from Satan's bondage can be brought to a needy world.

(G) *The Hand Of God To Deliver*

Moses now had to learn to trust God's deliverance against the stubbornness of Pharaoh. He had to discover personally for himself that there was no power too great, no enemy too strong, and no situation too difficult for the Lord to deliver him from.

In our own lives we can find certain situations stubbornly refuse to change, even though we may have cried out to God and waited, expecting a breakthrough for a long time. This can be so in our health, emotions, relationships, finances, ministry, church, the area of our own local mission field, or in our nation that seems so hard and difficult spiritually. When there is a delay and our prayers don't appear to be answered we can sink under the discouragement and disappointment of this.

As Moses goes forward to bring deliverance to Israel from Pharaoh, a whole catalogue of miracles occur one after the other. God begins to demonstrate His power to deliver in Exodus chapter 7 through to 12. The River Nile is turned to blood. There come plagues of frogs, gnats and flies. Cattle begin to die, sore boils afflict people's bodies, hail, locusts and thick darkness come upon the land, and the first-born son of every Egyptian is struck down dead. All this happens just as God had said to Moses and he not only witnesses this, but he is the instrument through which it all takes place. As a result, after many long years in captivity, Pharaoh lets God's people go.

(H) *The Guidance Of God*
The next lesson for Moses is not to be guided just by his own experience or even the expertise and opinions of others alone. Every single step that he takes must be by the direction of the Lord.

The first thing that happened for Moses and the Israelites, as soon as they came out of Egypt, was a pillar of fire by night, and cloud by day, led them through the wilderness. (Exodus 13:21). Whenever the pillar of fire or the cloud stopped they knew that God had stopped, and so they made camp. As soon as either of these began to move, they understood that God was on the move, so they immediately broke camp and moved also.

People frequently get into confusion and trouble simply because they are not following God's will. How often we make decisions without any reference to the Lord, and without committing our way to Him, then we are puzzled as to why our plans do not succeed. The Bible says,
>*"The steps of a good man are ordered by the Lord....."*
>   (Psalm 37:23, AV).
And again in Proverbs 3:6 it says,
>*"In all thy ways acknowledge Him, and He shall direct thy paths."*   (AV).
He is able to get us from where we are, to where He wants us to be, but we have to look to Him as our friend and trust in His care for our lives.

(I) *Confidence In God's Help When Under Attack*
Invariably when we are walking in the centre of God's will and are seeking to follow His direction, it is then that trouble comes along. Once we have come out of bondage and are walking together with the Lord, the enemy will attempt to snatch us back. This is why God's word says,
>*"For freedom Christ has set us free; stand fast therefore, and do not submit again to a yoke of slavery."* (Galatians 5:1).

If we are not careful we can lose the freedom we have gained, because we are not alert and standing firm in our faith.

This was the danger now for Moses and the children of Israel. Their enemy, Pharaoh, was wanting to bring them back into captivity and bondage. In Exodus 14:5-30, we see that the Egyptian army had been sent to pursue them and return them back to Egypt. The added complication in this predicament was, not only were the enemy pursuing from behind, but the Red Sea was in front of them, and they were sandwiched in the middle! They were in a hopeless situation where there was no way out.

Into this crisis Moses steps forward, and we notice he is a changed man now. This isn't the same person we saw at the beginning of the process; he has come a long way and has learnt to *'know'* his God. He speaks up as though he had been doing this kind of thing all his life and says,

> *".... Fear not, stand firm and see the salvation of the Lord, which He will work for you today; for the Egyptians whom you see today, you shall never see again. The Lord will fight for you, and you have only to be still."*

(Exodus 14:13&14).

Imagine the reassurance and confidence this must have brought to all those people who were gripped by fear.

This is just what God wants every Christian to be like. There are people all around us in life who feel trapped by their circumstances. They are facing insurmountable problems, feeling helpless and hopeless, and it seems as though there is no way out for them. God doesn't want us to go to such people with a 'sermon,' or simply express nice platitudes. He wants us to be able to speak the word of the Lord into their circumstances. Such a task is not possible any other way than from out of our relationship with God, otherwise what we say will be just a lot of 'hot air'.

(J) *God's Provision For Every Need*

The Red Sea is parted by God and, as Moses and the children of Israel walk through, their enemy is destroyed and they are saved. The process still hasn't finished yet for Moses though, the final thing that he has to learn is to have faith in the miraculous provision of God. He has 40 years in the wilderness to face now and the responsibility of looking after all Israel must have been immense. However, God proves Himself faithful to His people in providing for their every need. Throughout 40 years, food came down from heaven, water from out of the rock, and the people's clothes and shoes were not worn out in all that time.

We also need to have faith in God's provision, particularly in the wilderness times of our experience when it seems totally impossible that our needs will ever be met. It's relatively easy to believe and trust when everything is going well and there isn't much pressure. When times are difficult though, then we are really put to the test. It is during these occasions that we learn, out of our friendship with God, that He will provide because He is faithful!

In thinking over each of these different stages we can see what an incredible process knowing God was, for Moses. We would do well to ponder for ourselves how far we have come. Perhaps in doing so we'll identify an area where we've stopped along the way. Whatever the situation, let us have the discernment to recognise where we are, and the determination to move beyond that, to where God wants us to be.

Having looked at the "Prospect of Friendship with God" and seen that it is available to everyone, and having thought about the "Process of Friendship with God", let us now consider:

Thirdly, THE POTENTIAL OF FRIENDSHIP WITH GOD

The scripture we have based our thoughts on from Daniel 11:32 goes on to say, *"The people that do know their God, shall be **strong and do exploits.** "* We can see that this was clearly the case for Moses, but it is also true for each and every one of us. When we "know" our God then that friendship will give us a supernatural strength to stand strong, and an anointing to do great works for the Lord.

71

(A) *Standing*

In Ephesians 6:10 God's word says, *".... be strong in the Lord and in the strength of His might."* We need never again be tossed about by the circumstances of life; crumbling under the pressure of trials and yielding to temptation. We can stand strong just as Moses did. When our confidence is in God, rather than ourselves, then we are able to experience stability in our lives, in every way. David spoke of this when he said,

> *"Those who trust in the Lord are like Mount Zion, which cannot be moved, but abides for ever."* (Psalm 125:1).

From out of our relationship with the Lord we can be immovable. Our testimony will stand strong, just like a mountain against every storm. The friendship we have with God will help us overcome every difficulty, and enable us share with others that His exhortation to every believer is, *"Let the weak say I am strong."* (Joel 3:10, AV).

(B) *Stirred Into Action*

Not only shall we stand strong, but we will also be stirred into action, that is, to do 'great exploits!' The familiar words of John 14:12 are a constant challenge to us, and come to move us out into a new dimension of living. Jesus states,

> *"Truly, truly, I say unto you, he who believes in me, will also do the works that I do; and greater works than these will he do ......"*

Few Christians have really grasped the heart of what Jesus said here. The key that unlocks this amazing potential is found in the words, *".. he who believes in me...."* A strong belief can only ever come out of a strong relationship. This is the relationship that the Lord spoke of when He said,

> *"No longer do I call you servants, for the servant does not know what his master is doing; but I have called you friends, for all that I have heard from my Father I have made known to you."* (John 15:5).

(C) *Setting An Example*

Not only shall we be stirred into action, but we shall also set an example for others to follow. This brings us right back to where we started this chapter when we said, *"The depth of our relationship with the Lord will speak volumes to others."* Our friendship with God will set an example to our children, grandchildren, marriage partner, colleagues at work, neighbour, and one another in the church.

The impact of our lives on others will be just as significant as when Moses came down from Mount Sinai and everybody could see something had happened to him. He had spent time alone with God and the communion he had been having was noticed; not so much by what he said, but by how he looked. The Bible says of this incident,

> *"Moses did not know that the skin of his face shone because he had been talking with God."*   (Exodus 34:29b).

People will see in us the friendship that is possible to know with God, and it will stir their hearts to seek after the same reality for themselves.

The Lord is looking for people today who will place friendship with Him above everything else. These individuals may have few qualifications and little ability, but they have one thing going for them; the fact that they know their God. Let us be encouraged that what the Lord could do for Moses, with all his weaknesses and limitations, He can also do for us. We just need to be willing to move through each stage of the process He has for us, and be prepared to pay the cost of yielding everything to Him.

Chapter 5

The Divine Dynamic Of God's Word

An amusing incident is told about two little girls who quietly tiptoed past their elderly grandmother as she was avidly studying her Bible.
"Why is Granny always reading the Bible?" asked the one.
"Ssh!" whispered the other, *"We mustn't disturb her! She's cramming for her finals!"*

We may well smile, but God's word is of vital importance to every Christian, not just the elderly. This is because the foundation that our lives are built upon, from childhood to the grave, is either sinking sand or solid rock. There are only two options as far as God is concerned, and what determines this is our response to His word. Jesus illustrated this in the parable He gave to His disciples about the wise and foolish men in Matthew 7:24-27. Both these characters heard the same word, but only the one who put what was said into practice stood firm when the storms of adversity came against him. The person whose life collapsed with a mighty crash was the one who heard, but chose to ignore what he had been told.

The divine dynamic of God's word is that it not only *informs* but it also *transforms*. When we come to His word we should approach it expecting not simply to read *information* but to receive *impartation*! We receive something of the life and blessing of God to change us when we embrace what He has to say. This is why a life and church firmly based on the word of God is essential today, especially with all the false teaching, focus on experience and foolish antics that occur in the name of Christianity.

The first sixteen years of my own Christian experience were spent in a good Brethren Assembly in Exeter. Among the many excellent things they taught me there was a love for the scriptures. It is by holding God's word in high esteem that help is given to protect us against the dangers of:

(A) *False Teaching*

We are, without doubt, living in the last days and one of the warnings concerning this period is about false teaching. When speaking to Timothy about this danger Paul says,

"For the time is coming when people will no longer endure sound teaching, but having itching ears they will accumulate for themselves teachers to suit their own likings, and will turn away from listening to the truth and wander into myths." (2 Timothy 4:3&4).

We need to be so careful that we don't just accept anything and everything that a person says simply because we like their style of presentation or particular emphasis. Nor should we embrace everything that is preached merely because of the person's reputation. Their past success or present anointing is no protection against deception; only our own knowledge of God's word can give that. Some of the most anointed and respected ministries around today have not been without erroneous revelations at some time. Several that I've known personally have taught things as strange as the widely held notion that God the Father has a literal physical body, just like ours.

Also well documented, is one very prominent name known in this country who prophesied that revival would break out in Great Britain in October 1990, and spread throughout the nation. Then there was a Christian business-man who invested a lot of money in a book he had written, which taught that the Rapture of all believers would take place on 14th May, 1997. Such false teaching is only going to become more widespread in these end times. It is for this reason we need always to test everything against the plumbline of God's word. To do otherwise leaves us wide open to being deceived.

(B) *Focus On Experience*

We live in a day and age where there is an alarming preoccupation with experience and a pursuit after that which will give instant gratification and excitement. Experience would appear to be elevated in Church life today to such a level that it has ultimate authority as to the success of a meeting. Unless something dramatic or sensational has taken place then the meeting is deemed to have been a bit 'flat' and God is considered to have done nothing. Rather than letting the word of God judge our experience we allow our experience to judge His word.

I remember only too clearly being at a fellowship in the Midlands a few years ago where there was a tremendous move of the Holy Spirit during the worship. God was ministering to many people in a sovereign way as, one after another, lives were touched. This extended time of waiting on the Holy Spirit meant there was no time left for me to preach. I had no problem with that; in fact in over 20 years full-time ministry the same thing has happened probably 6 or 7 times. When this occurs I welcome it and it is the most marvellous sight. However, on this particular occasion, one of the elders came to me at the end of the meeting and said, *"Wasn't that wonderful! It would be tremendous if it were like this every week, then we wouldn't need the preaching of God's word!"*

While I appreciate what this man was trying to say, the deception and danger is obvious. Once we become focussed on experience and the latest 'manifestations' our attention is then diverted away from the importance of God's word, and onto what is happening to ourselves.

(C) *Foolish Antics*

The natural progression now, once we replace *sound doctrine* with *subjective desires*, is that anything and everything can take place in the Church. Simply give it the context of religious jargon, or charismatic hype and foolish antics begin to follow. I thank God for all He has done in recent years as His Holy Spirit has moved across the Church, bringing renewal and a much needed refreshing. Sometimes though, you can be in certain meetings and it's just like watching a circus performance, with a ring master orchestrating the spectacle! I've been long enough in the ministry to know when manipulation by the person leading or preaching is taking place, and some of the antics that go on are almost beyond belief.

The antics of manipulation is not the preserve of just the meeting though. Only a few days ago a most unusual letter, which was a circular from a well-known Christian ministry, came through my letter box. This was from one of the so-called 'Prosperity teachers,' (many of whom I greatly respect). It was encouraging Christians through a very cleverly worded text to believe for every bill and financial agreement, (including their mortgage), to be paid. The minister had enclosed some adhesive labels, with the words, *"Paid in full"* on, and these were to be attached to each household bill. Then these were to be posted to him and, on a given date, he would have a *"burning, thanksgiving service"* of everyone's debts. Before this took place though, the individual was instructed to send a cheque, amounting to 10% of the whole debt, to his organisation!

Once we begin to deviate from the teaching of scripture, and the sound principles of God's word, onto the subtle schemes of man, then a spirit of deception overtakes us, sending us down all sorts of 'dead end' streets.

God wants His people to be stable and strong, not as James describes, *"Tossed to and fro by every wind of doctrine."* (James 1:6). When we look at the New Testament Church in the book of Acts we see that although they had been baptised in the Holy Spirit, seen outstanding miracles, and had spoken with *"other tongues"*, the result wasn't a subjective slide into experience. One of the first things that happened was, *"They devoted themselves to the apostles teaching..."* (Acts 2:42). Their new experience of God gave them a greater love for His word.

Please don't mistake where I'm coming from. I am totally Pentecostal, thoroughly charismatic and completely evangelical. I believe in, and preach with a passionate conviction, renewal, restoration and revival. However, I am convinced we cannot afford to neglect or treat lightly the importance of scripture. What is so necessary in our lives today, particularly if we are to realise our full potential, is a deep commitment to God's word.

This attitude is encouraged by Jesus when He said,
"Man shall not live by bread alone, but by every word that proceeds from the mouth of God." (Matthew 4:4).

We must honour the importance of God's word, be hungry for what He has to say, and apply it in our daily experience. This isn't a dull adherence to the letter of the law bringing formalism and an attitude of legalism. Rather it is a delight and dependence in God's word bringing liberty and life! David best sums up this life; and his words express the potential that can be realised when he wrote in Psalm 1:1-3,
*"Blessed is the man who walks not in the counsel of the wicked, nor stands in the way of sinners, nor sits in the seat of scoffers; but his delight is in the law of the Lord and on His law he meditates day and night. He is like a tree planted by streams of water, - (*Strength*), that yields its fruit in its season, - (*Fruitfulness*), and its leaf does not wither. - (*Consistency*). In all that he does he prospers."- (*Success*).*

These four characteristics of being strong, productive, consistent and successful come as a natural matter of course to the person whose *"delight is in the law of the Lord."*

Our love for God's word is developed as we appreciate the divine quality and activity inherent in what God has to say. The divine dynamic is that God's word Revives, Reveals and it Reproduces after its own kind. This is what the writer to the Hebrew Christians had to say about it;
"For the word of God is living and active, sharper than any two-edged sword, piercing to the division of soul and spirit, of joints and marrow, and discerning the thoughts and intentions of the heart. And before Him no creature is hidden, but all are open and laid bare to the eyes of Him with whom we have to do." (Hebrews 4:12&13).

Firstly, GOD'S WORD REVIVES

To the weary and discouraged and those facing disappointment or frustration, God's word is, *"living and active"*. This was the clear conviction of one open-air preacher that I heard of. He was concerned to draw a crowd and get the attention of the indifferent passers-by, so he came up with a very imaginative idea. He took off his hat and placed it on the ground in the centre of the precinct, then discreetly slipped his Bible underneath. With great theatrical effect he then began pointing down at his hat and shouted excitedly at the top of his voice, *"It's alive! - It's alive! - It's alive!"*

Within seconds a large attentive crowd had gathered, and were watching the hat with great curiosity. The preacher then knelt carefully down and, reaching under his hat, he quickly pulled out his Bible and proceeded to preach about the living word of God!

The wonderful reality is that God's word is not simply a history book, or merely a helpful moral code of conduct. God's word is alive and brings revival! There is a divine dynamic in the scriptures that when imparted into situations which appear barren, even dead and beyond change, they bring a resurrection of hope. This was the case when the prophet Ezekiel received a vision from God about the state of the nation of Israel. In God's sight, because of their sinfulness, they were like a valley full of dry bones scattered everywhere, serving no useful purpose. But then came the command from God that was to change them from this state of death to new life. Ezekiel was told to prophesy to the bones and say to them, *"O dry bones, hear the word of the Lord .... "* (Ezekiel 37:4).

This same resurrection of hope transforms people everywhere as they listen and respond to the word of the Lord. Change comes into broken relationships, shattered hopes, frustrated ministries, empty lives, and hardened hearts. Because God's word is *"living and active"* it is right up-to-date and relevant to every situation, at all times, in all places and for all people.

No matter how great the darkness might be, the confidence we can have is that,

"The entrance of God's word brings light."   (Psalm 119:130).

I remember receiving a letter from someone who had been in the ministry for many years, who was grateful for the renewing power of God's word. He had ordered a copy of my book "Consistent Christian Living", that spoke about the importance of the scriptures in overcoming life's daily trials, and this is what he said:

"I must write and tell you of the circumstances prevailing on receipt of your book. I had decided that this life was no longer worth living. Having made a cup of tea I put two boxes of tablets on the table, thought over my life and ministry and decided to take the tablets.

Then on hearing the postman, I idly picked up the package that had just come through the door. Without much thought I tore it open and your book fell out, knocking the tablet boxes off the coffee table. The Lord lit a candle in the darkness of my heart as I began to read about God's word, and I simply sat and wept. But for His encouragement I know I would not be here today."

It's important to remember that no circumstance we can ever find ourselves in, will ever be able to stop us hearing God. No matter how big our problem might be, it can never cut us off from receiving God's word. This is seen in the life of Jeremiah the prophet. He had stood faithfully for God, speaking out against the unrighteousness in his nation, and as a result, he was thrown into prison. This is what we read, though, of his predicament,

"The word of the Lord came to Jeremiah a second time, while he was still shut up in the court of the guard."

(Jeremiah 33:1).

We must learn to expect God to speak into our situations, even when we appear to still be bound by difficult circumstances.

God's word is never passive, it is *"active"*, always doing something. There is a supernatural activity that takes place as His word is received. It brings to pass His will in us. There is a creative power bringing into our experience that which was not previously there. It actively creates faith, peace, confidence, joy, freedom etc.

God's word is able to bring cleansing into guilt, healing into sickness, deliverance into bondage, victory into failure, gladness into sorrow, guidance into uncertainty, and hope into discouragement. This is why God says of His word,

> "…. it shall not return to me empty, but it shall accomplish that which I purpose, and prosper in the thing for which I sent it." (Isaiah 55:11).

King David had a deep love and appreciation for God's word. He didn't see it as dull, dry, and unappealing as some do today. Because he believed in the divine dynamic of creative activity that was in the word he said,

> "The law of the Lord is perfect, reviving the soul; the testimony of the Lord is sure, making wise the simple; the precepts of the Lord are right, rejoicing the heart; the commandment of the Lord is pure, enlightening the eyes; the fear of the Lord is clean, enduring for ever; the ordinances of the Lord are true, and righteous altogether." (Psalm 19:7-9).

The creative activity going on here really is amazing. God's word: revives the soul, makes wise the simple, rejoices the heart, enlightens the mind, and endures for ever. When we think about this, our hearts ought to cry out to God, "Lord I need more of that activity in my life!"

Secondly, GOD'S WORD REVEALS

Having looked at the encouragement God's word brings to us, we now need to consider the challenge that comes as well. In Hebrews chapter 4 the writer goes on to say that God's word is,

> "….. sharper than any two-edged sword, piercing to the division of soul and spirit, joints and marrow, and discerning the thoughts and intentions of the heart. And before Him no creature is hidden, but all are open and laid bare…."

The awesome fact is that no person is hidden from God. He knows every secret, every problem, every motive, every thought, and every painful experience that we've ever had. A few years ago, while ministering at a church in Essex, I met someone who illustrated this fact in a tremendous way in her own life. Among those who came forward for prayer at the meeting was an attractive young woman who'd been leading the worship that morning. She said that she wanted to give her life to God in 'full time' Christian service and so we prayed with her to encourage her.

After the meeting she shared the most remarkable testimony with me. Only eleven months earlier this woman was not a Christian, far from it. On New Year's Eve of 1996 she was sitting in the foyer of a hotel as a so-called 'high class' call-girl, waiting to pick up a client. Her life had spiralled out of control since she was a young girl, largely due to the fact that as a child, her father, who was a minister of religion, had sexually abused her. Since that trauma her only feeling towards religion was anger. In growing up and turning her back on God she became a nude model, made over fifty hard-core pornographic videos and also worked as a 'table top' dancer in night clubs.

As she sat in the hotel waiting for her client, a Christian man walked in from off the street and, although he had never met her before, he went straight up to her and said just two things. His words were, *"I want you to know that God loves you and God is not to blame for the pain of your past."* This pierced her heart, and that same night she gave her life to Christ! So sure was she of the change which had occurred that, at 3.00 a.m. the following morning, she destroyed all her videos, photographs, magazines and clothes associated with her former life, and thanked God that she was now a new person!

Not only was this woman overwhelmed by God's knowledge of her, but she was completely stunned that His word came via that obedient Christian man, like a *"sharp, two-edged sword."*

When we are reminded of God's knowledge of us it brings either great alarm, or great assurance, depending on where we are in our relationship with Him. Also, in seeking to walk in obedience to what He says, we discover that His word gives us great authority.

(A) *Great Alarm*

This is what we should feel if we are living contrary to God's word and there is sin and compromise in our life. Any area of unreality will cause us to feel troubled when we are reminded that God sees everything, and will not let us get away with living in a way that dishonours Him. In looking at the New Testament Church, this is what we find established right at its very beginning. When Ananias and Sapphira were giving the impression that they had surrendered all to the Lord, their pretence was quickly exposed by Peter. He spoke the prophetic word of God to reveal their sin and they both dropped down dead! The alarm this brought is seen in Acts 5:11:

"And great fear came upon the whole church, and upon all who heard of these things."

Again we see how God's knowledge of us should cause concern if there is hypocrisy in our lives when we read about the Church at Corinth. All manner of carnality was going on there, yet they were coming to worship and taking communion as though it didn't matter. God's word through the Apostle Paul though, made clear to them that their sinfulness would be judged. He said,

"For any one who eats and drinks without discerning the body eats and drinks judgement upon himself. That is why many of you are weak and ill, and some have died."

(1 Corinthians 11:29&30).

Like a surgeon's knife, God's word is *"sharper than any two-edged sword."* It reveals the root of the problem and cuts away that which is damaging to our lives. This activity, therefore, of God's word should be seen as an expression of His loving mercy and not His wrath towards us.

(B) *Great Assurance*

Being reminded of God's knowledge of us can also bring a great sense of security into our lives, if we are in a right relationship with

Him and are seeking to live by faith in what His word reveals. Throughout the scriptures, God's word reveals the wonderful fact that He is for us and not against us. It shows us His protective hand watching over our lives and His provision to meet our every need.

If we are aware that God sees us in times of trouble, He notices when we are afraid, and understands when we are in need, then this should bring us tremendous comfort. This personal security is what the hymn writer must have felt when he penned the words, "Blessed assurance Jesus is Mine!"

King David also appreciated the assurance he received from being aware that his life was known to God. He said,

"He will not let your foot be moved, He who keeps you will not slumber. Behold, He who keeps Israel will neither slumber nor sleep. The Lord is your keeper; the Lord is your shade on your right hand. The sun shall not smite you by day, nor the moon by night. The Lord will keep you from all evil; He will keep your life. The Lord will keep your going out and your coming in from this time forth and forever more."

(Psalm 121:3-8).

We can only ever have this assurance when we, *"live by every word that proceeds from the mouth of God."* To ignore, or treat God's word lightly, is as foolish as for a sick man to ignore the doctor's advice, or someone who is lost to disregard the signposts standing in front of him.

(C) *Great Authority*

Sometimes God's word reveals failure in us as we compare our experience with what He says we can be, but exposing our weakness is not ultimately God's purpose. His word also reveals how we can overcome and live victoriously, regardless of what tries to defeat us.

Jesus lived in total victory over temptation and trials because He was able to meet each attack, confidently saying, *"It is written..."* (Matthew 4: verses 4,7&10). It is of utmost importance therefore, if we are to live with the same measure of authority and confidence, that we also know what is written.

The necessity of studying God's word and applying it in life's situations cannot be over-emphasised if we really want to make the most of our potential.

At the same time that Joshua was to take on the great responsibility of leadership, with all its pressures and challenges, God instructed him very clearly. He said,

> *"This book of the law shall not depart out of your mouth,*
> *but you shall meditate on it day and night, that you might be*
> *careful to do according to all that is written in it; for then you*
> *shall make your way prosperous, and then you shall have*
> *good success."*   (Joshua 1:8).

Before the prophet, Ezra, could make known to Israel God's word, and share the Lord's direction with those in need, he had to make sure that he was first clear on what God's word said to him; then that he was applying it to his own life. His commitment to this is seen in that he,

> *".... set his heart to study the law of the Lord, and to do it,*
> *and to teach His statutes and ordinances in Israel."*
>   (Ezra 7:10).

This same priority of knowing the scriptures should be in the hearts of all those who want to be their best for God. It is not something that is just an Old Testament principle, but a clear requirement of all those who desire to serve the Lord.

When Paul was training his young disciple Timothy he said,

> *"Do your best to present yourself to God as one approved,*
> *a workman who has no need to be ashamed, rightly handling*
> *the word of truth."*   (2 Timothy 2:15).

The very thing that blunts the cutting edge of our testimony and restricts the great potential we have is a neglect of this requirement.

Thirdly, GOD'S WORD REPRODUCES

Having looked at the encouragement and challenge that God's word brings, the final aspect to consider is the potential it places within us. When God's word starts as a seed planted in the good soil of our hearts, it grows and produces much fruit. In fact the exciting thing is that it reproduces after its own kind.

I remember the time, a few years ago now, that my younger daughter came home from her junior school with her latest project. She had in her hands a small flower-pot, filled with soil which contained a sunflower seed. As she showed it to me there wasn't much to see, just a tiny green shoot peering out of the soil. It wasn't really that impressive, but I encouraged her and said how well she had done.

A few months had passed when one afternoon she brought home this pot again. I'm not sure how she made her way back from school but she did, and when she walked in through the door I couldn't believe what I was looking at. Tightly holding the pot, she proudly presented her plant to me. This time, rather than a small insignificant shoot peering up at me, there was an 8ft. sunflower looking down on me!

The potential that was inside the small seed had grown and blossomed out in all its glory. Its life and nature had reproduced itself far beyond my expectations. The same miracle is true with God's word. As we live by faith in the scriptures, the divine nature of God Himself is reproduced in our lives in the following ways:

(A) *Our Character*
The likeness of Jesus is reproduced in us as we apply the promises God has made and the knowledge of Him that we receive from His word in our daily experience. Peter refers to this when he says,
> *"His divine power has granted to us all things that pertain to life and godliness, through the knowledge of Him who called us to His own glory and excellence, by which He has granted to us His precious and very great promises, that through these you may escape the corruption that is in the world because of passion, and become partakers of the divine nature".* (2 Peter 1:3&4).

Our character is shaped and made by all of life's experiences and choices, but also in a very real sense we will become what we behold. That which we focus on will have a controlling influence in our life. If we therefore choose to let our hearts be fixed on God's word, then we will be transformed in our character to be like Jesus. The apostle Paul understood this when he said,

> "..... we beholding the glory of the Lord, are being changed into His likeness from one degree of glory to another ...." (2 Corinthians 3:18).

(B) *Our Conduct*

The way that Jesus acted and reacted will become part of our own lifestyle, which is why we can expect to do the works He did and greater works. This can certainly be understood in terms of supernatural power, but also in terms of works of compassion to the poor and destitute, the weak and the vulnerable. Once God's word is in us we have the potential of responding to situations as He did; selflessly giving our time to help others.

When we consider the parable of the Good Samaritan with which Jesus challenged the religious people of His day, we see actions speaking louder than words or good intentions. The conduct that is expected of followers of Christ is that we are a friend to all those around us who are in need. With the Good Samaritan Jesus taught that our action needs to be practical, even at personal cost to ourselves. In referring to the conduct of the Samaritan, those hearing His words were left with the challenge to, *"Go and do likewise."* (Luke 10:37b).

(C) *Our Conversation*

The way we speak is part of our high calling to have a manner of life worthy of the gospel. Paul says,

> *"Let no evil talk come out of your mouths, but only such as is good for edifying, as fits the occasion, that it may impart grace to those who hear."* (Ephesians 4:29).

What we say imparts something to others. When we live by His word, then His word through us will have the effect of imparting life into dead situations, creating in others that which was not previously there, and bring a sharp, cutting edge to our ministry that will release those who are bound by sin and Satan's power.

When we previously looked at Psalm 19:7-9 we observed the divine activity these words spoke of. Notice now the divine adjectives that are also expressed. It speaks of how the law of the Lord is *"perfect"*, the testimony of the Lord is *"sure"*, the precepts of the Lord are *"right"*, the commandments of the Lord are *"pure"*, and the ordinances of the Lord are *"true and righteous"*. If our heart is filled with that which is perfect, sure, right, pure, true and righteous, then we can be certain of having a positive effect on others with what we say.

Jesus taught about the importance of being filled with the right things when He said, *"…. for out of the abundance of the heart the mouth speaks."* (Luke 6:45b).

In an age where experience has become a preoccupation with some people, and commitment a neglected discipline, a love for God's word is essential if we are to be stable and strong, protected from deception and more able to minister to others.

The divine dynamic of God's word in our life will not only inform, but transform us completely as it **Revives**, **Reveals**, and **Reproduces** itself in our lives.

Chapter 6

The Manifest Presence Of God

One of the few places in the world where the air is as clean as it was thousands of years ago is the South Pole. Constant winds keep out pollution and germs, and the climate discourages the growth of native viruses. It sounds like the healthiest place on earth. Why is it, therefore, that no one lives there? The reason is, because it's just too cold; the temperature can drop to -126 degrees Fahrenheit!

Living in the right atmosphere and environment spiritually, directly affects our ability to grow as Christians. If we are to develop into all we have the potential of being then it is essential that we are conscious of, and dependent upon, our need for God's presence. The Bible says,
"In Him we live and move and have our being".   (Acts 17:28).

We have not been called to live in sickness, depression, fear, rejection or any other problem, but to live and walk with a deep awareness of God. This doesn't mean we'll never be sick or depressed and that we'll never have problems; but it does mean that when we know His abiding presence, we'll have a new inner strength to help us overcome so that we can reach our full potential.

One of the saddest verses in the Bible refers to man's original awareness of God's presence. The scriptures record,
"They heard the sound of the Lord God walking in the garden in the cool of the day, and the man and his wife hid themselves from the presence of the Lord...."   (Genesis 3:8).
What a tragic verse this is. Here we have God seeking fellowship; wanting to draw near to man, and yet as His presence is revealed, the creation He loves turns away and hides from Him. The manifest presence of God will always have the effect of either bringing communion, or conviction. We are either drawn into a closer

relationship with Him, or we become so convicted that we want to turn away and hide.

People are very good at hiding today. Just recently, while taking a meeting in Suffolk, a very plump lady shared with me that she was struggling with her weight problem. She admitted, though, that she was using her size to hide behind, as protection from the unwanted attention of men. As a child she had been sexually abused from the age of 3 to 15years by her father and grandfather. Fear, from this trauma, created in her mind the irrational belief that if she was overweight then no man would bother her.

Some people hide behind a smile that covers up their deep hurts and needs. Others hide behind the words of songs they sing in worship. They express words of intimacy and love towards God, and yet little reality of the things they're saying is in their lives. Some hide behind the busyness of activities. Looking very impressive they are always rushing around, even in the 'work of the Lord,' but so busy that they haven't got time to be alone with God. Then there are those who hide behind their seating position in the congregation. Each week the same seat is chosen, usually towards the back, so they don't get too near, or too involved in anything that might happen in the meeting. Other people hide behind their relationships, whether it's with their marriage partner or their young children, so nothing too much is expected of them personally.

A new visitation of God's glory and power is coming to the Church in these days, drawing people into a place of reality and demonstrating that there is a vast difference between the omnipresence and manifest presence of the Lord. God is omnipresent in that His presence is all around us, at all times, wherever we are. The Psalmist spoke of this when he said,

"Where can I go from your Spirit? Where can I flee from your presence? If I go up to the heavens, you are there; if I make my bed in the depths, you are there."

(Psalm 139:7&8, NIV).

This is the general presence of God that is everywhere at one and the same time. There are, though, those 'special' times as well; those wonderful occasions when the presence of God becomes so specific, almost tangible, and we know that He is amongst us. Jacob woke up to this discovery one day, at a place called Bethel. He said of that experience,

"Surely the Lord is in this place; and I did not know it."

(Genesis 28:16b).

The revealed presence of God spoken of in Genesis 3:8 is something I've puzzled over for a long time now, especially where it says, *"They heard the sound of the Lord God walking in the garden"*. What exactly did they hear? Was it the rustle of the bushes as God moved along? Was it the ground quaking, as it were, under giant footsteps as He made His approach? We don't know exactly what they heard, nor do we know quite how God revealed Himself, but what we do know is this; it was unmistakable! They knew that it was God and there was no doubt whatsoever in their minds.

When we look further into the scriptures we see how clear and unmistakable the manifest presence of God is, in contrast to His general presence. In 2 Chronicles 5:13&14 we have the priests ministering in the temple, going through the ritual and routine of their religious duties. They were sincerely doing the same things they had always done, but on this occasion it was very different for them. We read,

".... the house of the Lord, was filled with a cloud, so that the priests could not stand to minister because of the cloud; for the glory of the Lord filled the house of God."

These people were flat on their faces because God's presence had broken in so powerfully that they could not stand.

Another amazing example is found in Exodus 19:16-20. Here God's people had come to Mount Sinai to meet with the Lord. There they experienced His presence in a way they would never forget. Moses says of that event:

"On the morning of the third day there were thunders and lightnings and a thick cloud upon the mountain, and a very loud trumpet blast, so that all the people who were in the camp trembled. Then Moses brought the people out of the camp to meet God; and they took their stand at the foot of the

*mountain. And Mount Sinai was wrapped in smoke, because
the Lord descended upon it in fire; and the smoke of it went
up like the smoke of a kiln, and the whole mountain quaked
greatly. And as the sound of the trumpet grew louder and
louder, Moses spoke, and God answered him in thunder. And
the Lord came down upon Mount Sinai, to the top of the
mountain ... ."*

In this incident we have thunder and lightning, thick cloud, smoke
and fire, people trembling and a very loud trumpet blast. God's
manifest presence was clear and powerful. There was certainly no way
any person could nod off to sleep in that meeting; no chance of anyone
getting bored during this encounter with the Lord!

In the New Testament the manifest presence of God is equally
clear. On the very first day that the Church came into being we have a
memorable experience in Acts 2:2. There we read,

*"And suddenly a sound came from heaven like the rush of
a mighty wind ... ."*

This was no ordinary wind, it was God's glory and power breaking in
and changing the lives of His people. Then in Acts 2:3 a visible
expression of God's presence with His disciples is seen as, *"Tongues of
fire rested on each of them"*. Also, in Acts 4:31, the believers were
praying together when God suddenly came among them and the whole
building was shaken with the power of His presence.

Again in Acts 10 there is a remarkable example of the presence of
the Lord affecting people's lives. Here, a group of believers had come
together to hear the word of God being spoken by Peter. As he is
preaching, suddenly the presence of God comes upon every one
listening, and they all spontaneously break out in tongues, worshipping
the Lord:

*"While Peter was still saying this, the Holy Spirit fell on
all who heard the word. And the believers from among the
circumcised who came with Peter were amazed, because the
gift of the Holy Spirit had been poured out even on the
Gentiles. For they heard them speaking in tongues and
extolling God"*. (verses 44-46).

Those gathered together didn't wait for Peter to finish his message, or for someone to strike up a chorus, they just cut right across his sermon and burst out praising God! If this happened more often in our meetings today then our services would be very different, and certainly more interesting!

Throughout the book of Acts an acute sense of God's presence is experienced on numerous occasions, with incidents of healings, deliverances and conversions. It was this that gave the Church its vibrant life, causing it to stand out in the community and capture the interest of those who were unbelievers. In fact there is one phrase found in the book of Acts that bears testimony to the impact it made on others:
"About that time there arose no little stir concerning the Way."
(Acts 19:23).

This was so, not because a great preacher or talented music group was there, nor because a large crusade had been organised; God was there, and everyone knew it! This is what our nation needs to see today; a sovereign move of Almighty God bringing a revelation of His glory. There can be no substitute for this and it will come through the lives of those who have learnt to depend on, hunger after, and be open to the presence of the Lord.

As we think about the need we have for this same sense of the Lord's presence in our lives, let us consider:

Firstly, WHY KNOWING GOD'S PRESENCE IS ESSENTIAL
Not until we begin to see how important the manifest presence of God is among His people will we start to seek after that reality? Some of the benefits this brings to us are:

(A) *Distinctiveness To Our Witness*
Rather than having a bland, boring, irrelevant testimony and living a life of mediocrity, we have been called to stand out and be noticed as different. This distinctiveness isn't seen because of the clothes we wear, the size of Bible we carry, or the religious jargon that we talk. It isn't by the style of worship in our meetings, or because of the name of our

95

denomination either. We become distinctive because the presence of the Lord is with us. This is what Moses was referring to when he said:

> *"For how shall it be known that I have found favour in thy sight, I and thy people? Is it not in thy going with us, so that we are distinct, I and thy people, from all other people that are upon the face of the earth?"* (Exodus 33:16).

God doesn't want us simply to be like everyone else; for there to be no difference between ourselves and those who are unsaved. We are unique; He wants us to be like a *".... city set on a hill that cannot be hid"*. (Matthew 5:14). What made the New Testament Christians so unlike the religious of their day was simply that God was evidently with them. It seemed every time they preached, a miracle occurred; each time they made known the gospel, something remarkable happened.

Regrettably it would appear we have drifted a long way from that kind of experience. When we look at Church life now and compare it with how things were then, we are left with the unavoidable conclusion that there is a huge difference, and the one glaring characteristic missing today is the manifest presence of God.

(B) *Reassurance In The Face Of Responsibility*

We all have responsibilities in some area and to varying degrees, whether we are at home, at work, or in the ministry, and this at times can bring us under great pressure. We can become very aware of our own weaknesses and limitations and be overwhelmed by the tasks given to us. It is at such times we need the reassurance that only the presence of the Lord can give us.

This was the case for Joshua when he was faced with the enormous responsibility of taking over the leadership of Israel from Moses. The end of an outstanding era had come; Moses was dead and now Joshua had to continue the work. With human nature being what it is, people must have made comparisons between the two men. Joshua could easily have felt intimidated and, to some extent, tempted to doubt his adequacy for the job. However, God speaks to him and says,

"No man shall be able to stand before you all the days of your life; as I was with Moses, so I will also be with you; I will not fail you or forsake you." (Joshua 1:5).

This is what we need to hear as we face the pressures and responsibilities of each day; God's presence with us, and not our ability, is our guarantee for success.

(C) *Security In Times Of Trouble*

The trials of life are very real for each of us. When we feel trapped by difficult problems, a darkness of fear and gloom can begin to descend. In such situations it is the presence of God that brings great security, just as it did for David. He said,

"Even though I walk through the valley of the shadow of death, I will fear no evil; for thou art with me...."
(Psalm 23:4).

David was the man who stood against Goliath, wrestled with a bear, tore apart a lion with his own hands; it was David that overthrew armies. In all his exploits he was secure because he knew an abiding sense of the Lord's presence.

Isaiah also knew the same security in times of adversity. He was confident because God had said to him,

"When you pass through the waters I will be with you; and through the rivers, they shall not overwhelm you; when you go through fire you shall not be burned, and the flame shall not consume you." (Isaiah 43:2).

Joseph is probably the clearest example of the difference God's presence makes in times of trouble. This young man had been given a dream from the Lord that one day people were going to bow down before his greatness. Soon after receiving this, though, he was rejected by his brothers and sold into slavery. So rather than being in a position of great authority, he was just a slave for another man. However, in spite of the fact that trouble had conspired against him and was standing between him and the fulfilment of God's promise, we read,

97

"The Lord was with Joseph, and he became a successful man; and he was in the house of his master the Egyptian, and his master saw that the Lord was with him, and that the Lord caused all that he did to prosper in his hands."

(Genesis 39:2&3).

You would think that it surely couldn't get any worse for Joseph, but the next thing that occurs is that he is falsely accused by his master's wife of attempted rape and thrown in prison. With everything looking as though it had fallen apart for him we read,

"But the Lord was with Joseph and showed him steadfast, love and gave him favour in the sight of the keeper of the prison." (Genesis 39:21).

Joseph wasn't in the position of greatness yet; he was still in the prison cell, but because he knew the presence of the Lord he was secure, even in adversity. His faith was in God's faithfulness and so eventually God led him through the valley of the shadow of death and raised him up to be governor over all Egypt; second only to Pharaoh. As we rest in His presence we also can be encouraged that the promise we have received, and the dream that is yet to be fulfilled for us will come to pass, regardless of what tries to delay or destroy it.

(D) *Fulfilment In Our Daily life*

There are times we can feel spiritually dry and frustrated, left thinking that there must be more to our Christian experience than what we have known. When our enthusiasm seems to have gone and dissatisfaction has crept in, we need to go back to the scriptures and see what has been promised.

Fulfilment is guaranteed to those who set their hearts on God. If, however, we get distracted in our walk with the Lord and are seeking anyone or anything else before Him, then we will always feel dissatisfied and disappointed. Look what happens, though, when you live and move and have your being in Him. David says,

"Take delight in the Lord, and He will give you the desires of your heart." (Psalm 37:4).

It is in choosing the presence of God as the source of all our fulfilment, to meet every need, that our lives are kept spiritually fresh. We can then be content and grow, even in circumstances that are hard and difficult. The two things we can be sure of when we keep God, rather than our 'needs,' as the focus of our life are His perfect provision and His perfect timing.

Secondly,
THINGS THAT CLOUD OUR EXPERIENCE OF HIS PRESENCE
God wants to draw near to us and make Himself known, therefore, if we don't experience this it is because something is in the way. For example, on a summer's day when the sun is shining, life looks better and people tend to feel much more positive. We think, feel and speak differently as we enjoy the presence of the sunshine upon our lives. If, however, a dark cloud suddenly comes across the sun, we immediately lose the blessing of the sunshine, and a cold greyness comes in its place. The sun hasn't moved; it's just that something has come in-between, affecting our experience of its presence.

It is the same in our relationship with God. He is closer to us than our very breath, but sometimes we don't experience His presence, because something has come across our relationship to rob us of that blessing. Some of these things could be:

(A) *Worldliness*
This can be generally understood to mean an attitude or activity which reflects a lowering of godly standards, and it will always affect our relationship with the Lord. The Bible says,
> *"Unfaithful creatures! Do you not know that friendship with the world is enmity with God?"* (James 4:4).

Throughout Christianity the term 'worldliness' has meant different things to different people. What one might consider sinful and ungodly, or just unhelpful, particularly in areas like fashion, music and entertainment, another may have no problem with. We cannot impose our standards on others. For some Christians of a past generation, going to the cinema, or watching television on Sunday was considered 'worldly'. Today's Christian is a little more relaxed about such things, but there's no doubt that with changing attitudes and standards, compromise has come into the Church, influencing our devotion to God.

When the Bible uses the phrase *"the world"*, in the context of warning against the danger of compromise, it refers to society organised apart from God. The command that is given is,

"Do not love the world or the things in the world. If anyone loves the world, love for the Father is not in him."

(1 John 2:15).

This verse shows us that when we set our desires on anything the world can offer for satisfaction, then it changes our love for God in a negative way. The attraction of anything that conflicts with God's word always makes us self-conscious rather than God-conscious, just as the 'forbidden fruit' did for Adam and Eve in the Garden of Eden. When there is compromise in our life, the presence of God makes us feel embarrassed and ashamed. If we are in a meeting and the power and presence of God begins to move upon people, then we immediately start to feel uncomfortable.

Any approach to God and desire to know His presence in a deeper way can only be achieved on the basis of absolute purity. This is why the Psalmist says,

"Who shall ascend to the hill of the Lord? And who shall stand in His holy place? He who has clean hands and a pure heart, who does not lift up his soul to what is false, ... such is the generation of those who seek Him, who seek the face of the God of Jacob." (Psalm 24:3-6).

Susanna Wesley, mother of John and Charles Wesley, gave some useful guidelines in relation to the problem of worldliness. These help determine the things we should avoid. She said,

"Whatever impairs our reason, hardens the tenderness of our conscience, obscures our vision of God, or dulls our relish for Spiritual things; that for me is sin."

Anything adversely affecting our relationship with the Lord must be renounced and repented of if we are to enjoy His presence.

(B) *Tunnel Vision*

Just like a horse wearing blinkers, some people have a very narrow way of looking ahead. They are so determined to stay 'on course' and not wander into anything that might be considered dangerous that they ignore any new revelation or experience that is going on around them. Their intention is admirable, but not if the direction they have set for themselves is taking them away from what God may be doing.

Such people hear reports of how the Lord is revealing Himself to others, but they reject what they hear as false. In doing this the Holy Spirit in their lives is grieved and the opportunity to know God's presence in a deeper way passes them by. If the unpredictable and unexpected happens in a meeting, some miss what God is doing simply because it doesn't fit into the way they see that things should be.

When something strange or unusual, that is outside their experience, occurs they say, *"I just don't understand the point of it"*. And again I've often heard people comment, *"God would never do anything that would make people look foolish"*. Those who make such remarks have not properly read their Bibles for the facts. God frequently does things that make no sense to us, even things that we would consider to be foolish. It isn't uncommon, either, to find God doing things that appear bizarre.

Ezekiel, for example, was told by God to lie on his left side for 390 days and then on his right side for 40 days, as some sort of prophetic, symbolic word to the people of Israel. (Ezekiel 4:4-6). Even stranger than this God said to Isaiah that he was to walk before the people naked and barefoot for 3 years! (Isaiah 20:2&3). Also, with Hosea the prophet, God told him that he was to take a wife for himself who was a prostitute. This wasn't a repentant or reformed sinner, but someone who was still living an immoral life! (Hosea 1:2).

In looking at Jesus we find that He did many strange and bizarre things that didn't make much sense; things that could well have been misunderstood and criticised. Today He would have been labelled *"The Spitting Preacher"* by some, because of healing a blind man by the unconventional means of spitting into dirt and placing the mixture onto his eyes. (John 9:1-7).

On another occasion, with a deaf and dumb person, Jesus not only spat, He also put His fingers in the man's ears! (Mark 7:32-35). These things are outside the vision of the person wearing spiritual blinkers and so they are unable to see what God is doing.

(C) *Pride*

This is another great blockage that is closely related to the previous point. When people have strong unbending opinions and are harshly critical, they are quick to make judgements and jump to the wrong conclusions. These attitudes come out of a spiritual pride that stands against anything which is contrary to their own ideas, so that there is no room for any other interpretation or way of thinking than their own.

Harsh, legalistic thinking is sadly very common in the Church today and is something that I come across frequently. While holding an open-air meeting in the centre of Leicester last year, a group of Christian gypsies came to speak to us after the meeting. They were warm and enthusiastic in their commitment to Christ and we had an encouraging time of fellowship together, at least until the head gypsy spoke up with a question. He asked, *"What do you think of all these reports we're hearing, about a new visitation of the Holy Spirit and strange manifestations in meetings?"*

I said to him that no doubt some of the things happening in this experience were of the flesh, and certain things were likely to be of a demonic origin. However, amongst it all there was a genuine, authentic move of the Holy Spirit that we ought to give thanks to God for.

His reaction to this was to rise up with a proud and arrogant attitude and say, *"I can't accept what is happening today, and I don't believe this is of the Holy Spirit!"*

His opinions were punctuated throughout with "I", "Me" and "My" and the good fellowship we'd been having only moments earlier was broken as he distanced himself from us. His manner became cold, suspicious and aggressive as he continued to attribute everything he'd heard of as a *"work of the devil!"*

(D) *Religious Traditions*

Not all religious traditions are wrong, but once they start to elevate themselves to the same level as God's word they develop into man's rules regarding religion and soon become a bondage to us. This is found in churches that express the attitude, *"We've always done it this way, so we're always going to do it this way"*. Once we begin to cling to a structure that has become inflexible, then it is a huge hindrance to God moving in any new or 'unscheduled' way.

In Matthew 15:6 Jesus addressed this specific problem when He said to the religious of His day,
" …. for the sake of you traditions, you have made void the word of God."

There are churches that have emptied God's word of its power by this error. Even some Pentecostal congregations are more bound by tradition than other denominations that we'd perhaps expect this problem in. Also, in some charismatic fellowships you can be in the meeting and you know exactly what is going to take place next. It has its own pattern and routine that has become predictable. The new structure, which replaced the previous one years ago, has itself become inflexible, so no one expects anything unusual to happen. The result is that we lose the spontaneity, excitement and freedom that once was there.

One of the great bondages today of religious tradition is 'clock watching'. In some places people seem more preoccupied with the time and their need to get back home at a certain hour, than honouring God and waiting upon Him.

I remember arriving at a Pentecostal Church in Yorkshire where this was the case. The Pastor, just before the meeting, said to me *"We start at 5.45 p.m. and there'll be some praise and worship, testimonies, the notices, a Bible reading, and a time of open prayer - then you can preach, but we finish at 7.00 p.m."*

As he said this, immediately I felt as though a straight-jacket had been put upon me.

They had just finished decorating the building and the clock, which used to hang in front of the preacher at the back of the hall, had been taken down. The Pastor, however, went out to a side room and brought this large clock back in. He explained that he was just going to put it up again so I could see when it was 7.00 p.m. Then he mentioned he would be sitting on the back row, underneath the clock, while somebody else led the meeting.

Eventually it came round for me to preach and, as I did, a tremendous anointing came upon the gathering. The presence of God became very evident and while I was speaking I noticed, at the back of the room, the pastor's hand slowly rise up toward the direction of the clock. He took it down, turned the hands back an hour, then put it on the wall again!

Many that night came forward for prayer and the move of God in the meeting was tremendous. After a while the pastor came out from one of the back-rooms he'd been in and said to me, *"I've been in my office sobbing my heart out. What God has done tonight is wonderful. I'm so glad that I didn't get in the way of what He wanted to do!"*

It is important for us all that our religious traditions, whatever they might be, do not hinder what the Holy Spirit wants to do. We ought always to have an expectancy for the unexpected as we gather together and simply let God be God among us.

Thirdly, KNOWING A GREATER SENSE OF GOD'S PRESENCE
Because God's word is clear and practical it only takes two verses to immediately show us how His presence can be a greater reality in our lives. This direction is given by James when he says,

> *"Submit yourselves therefore to God. Resist the devil and*
> *he will flee from you. Draw near to God and He will draw*
> *near to you …."*   (James 4:7&8).

(A) *Surrender Our Will*

The first thing we have to do is, for some, often the hardest one of all. James says, *"Submit yourselves therefore to God"*. So many people are too strong-willed for their own good. Of course we don't surrender our will to anyone or anything, but as far as God is concerned this is the first step to knowing Him. We must submit our opinions and will to His word and the moving of His Holy Spirit.

All our own preconceived ideas, predetermined plans and personal preferences must be laid to one side. Rather than making known that we don't agree with a certain thing, we need to have an openness of mind to say, *"Lord, I submit myself to whatever you want to do and however you want to move."*

There are those today who would do well to heed the advice of Jonathan Edwards, the great revivalist of the 18th Century. He once said, *"We ought not to limit God where He has not limited Himself."*

As we submit ourselves to the Lord, it means that we come before Him honestly and in reality. Where there have been things that have been a blockage we must be prepared to humble ourselves and admit them.

One lady, who was an elder's wife from a church in Cheshire, came to me at the end of the meeting and shared that she desperately needed prayer. She said that for two years she had been pretending and just going through the motions of church life. Her confession was, *"I've been wearing a mask and nobody but God is aware of this. I desperately want reality in my life!"*

As we prayed that morning, God touched her in a wonderful way and released her into a new consciousness of His presence. Discovering this reality was only possible, though, because she was prepared to submit herself to the convicting power of the Holy Spirit.

(B) *Stand Against The Enemy*

The next thing that James says is, *"Resist the devil and he will flee from you"*. Unless we stand against the enemy he will rob us of the prospect of knowing God in a deeper way, either through the lies that he feeds to us, or the emotions he stirs up. Frequently the fears and suspicions people hold are based on the lies and distortions of Satan that they've received. His strategy is to bring suspicion and division into the Church. He knows that if he can turn Christians against each other, then he can rob the Church of the blessing and power of God.

We must take a stand against the enemy also in terms of being his messengers. The way lies and half-truths are spread is often through the gossip, criticism, innuendo and the negative talk of other Christians.

Satan has many believers unwittingly assisting his work and in so doing they are hindering the work of God. These self-appointed 'Defenders of the Truth' publish newsletters, write articles and circulate videos that criticise other ministries. Such people are not only using their time in a negative way, but also are dividing the Church of God.

James brings a warning to these Christians when he speaks of the tongue as a,
> *".... restless evil, full of deadly poison. With it we bless the Lord and Father, and with it we curse men, who are made in the likeness of God."* (James 3:8&9).

It is time to unite and stand together as one, majoring on the things that we do agree with, rather than concentrating on those things we don't. This doesn't mean we are not to be discerning, or that we shouldn't 'test' prophecy, but it does mean we give no opportunity to the devil.

Paul warns about the danger that we can be to one another when he says, *"If you bite and devour one another, take heed that you are not consumed by one another"*. (Galatians 5:15).

(C) *Step Out And Start Seeking*
We should not passively sit in our churches and just expect one day that something will happen. God will not do it all; there is something we have to do. There must come from ourselves a response; some indication of our desire, which is why James says, *"Draw near to God*

and He will draw near to you". God looks for an openness in our lives and, when this is indicated, He then begins to draw near.

The same thought of taking action is brought out by David in Psalm 27:8. He understood that by acting upon God's direction then he would find the presence of the Lord. Because of this, we see in him a determination not to delay:

"Thou hast said, 'Seek ye my face'. My heart says to thee,
'Thy face, Lord, do I seek'."

It isn't enough just to hear the word of God; we have to open our lives to Him, also, and begin to draw near. The only way we can do this is when we come on the basis of His promise which says,

"For whoever would draw near to God must believe that
He exists and that He rewards those who seek Him."

(Hebrews 11:6b).

We also must come and approach Him with thankfulness. Many are robbed of their awareness of God's presence simply because they get distracted by grumbling and complaining. I've noticed that those who are always finding fault and being negative are the people who never have any evidence of God's presence with them in their daily walk. Such individuals, when talking to you, leave you drained and poorer for having been with them. We cannot experience and maintain the presence of God in our lives unless we are living with thankfulness in our hearts. This is why the psalmist said,

"Let us come into His presence with thanksgiving...."

(Psalm 95:2).

As we draw near to God we must do so with an earnest intent. This involves an attitude of heart, a discipline of mind, and a resolve of the will to seek after God. Very often we do not know a greater sense of the Lord's presence because we are not hungry enough for a move of God. Someone has rightly said, *"Spiritual fulfilment comes in the exact proportion to the intensity of our desire"*. The reason why people are not sufficiently hungry is because they have so many other priorities; other things that seem more attractive and more interesting than seeking the presence of God.

His presence should be of greater concern to us than getting on in business or succeeding in life. It should be more important than any relationship we're pursuing or the interests and hobbies that we hold dear; and more important than acquiring the material possessions others chase after. We constantly need to reassess our priorities and re-evaluate where we are before the Lord. The passion of David's heart is an example to us all. He said,

"For a day in thy courts is better than a thousand elsewhere."
(Psalm 84:10).

God in these days is '*Walking in the Garden of His Church*' and He is looking for closer fellowship with man. He is wanting to reveal His presence in a greater, more powerful way so that we will have a deeper dependence to live and move and have our being in Him. We can choose to settle for the general presence of God, and in doing so we will receive a measure of comfort from that. Alternatively, we can decide that more than anything else we want to know His personal manifest presence in our lives and also in our churches.

Chapter 7

Liberty In The Holy Spirit

Towering high above New York harbour, there can be seen the imposing figure of the Statue of Liberty. This stately lady with freedom's torch held high, stands as a symbol of 'faith in America' for all the oppressed of that land. While it certainly looks impressive, the statue, is of course, powerless in itself to change people's lives. The person of the Holy Spirit however is quite different; He directs us not to a statue or symbol but to a living Saviour, one who is active today, bringing liberty to all who are weary, bound and oppressed!

Just like a river of life, the Spirit of God is flowing across the world today in an amazing way, and multitudes are finding a new freedom that they never experienced before. What I am finding in these days is that never, in over twenty years of preaching, has there been a more exciting time to minister God's word. The Lord, by His Holy Spirit, is bringing an openness and responsiveness that I've not seen for a long time in this country. It is unusual now not to see God confirming His word in some remarkable way, even in the more reserved congregations.

An example of many such meetings was not long ago, whilst speaking at a traditional church in the north on the subject of the Holy Spirit. The atmosphere was extremely heavy and the service hard going, with the Pastor keeping a tight rein on the programme. We 'limped' through the choruses, one after the other, and as the evening 'progressed,' I remember thinking to myself, *"God, if you can do something here, you can do it anywhere!"* By the end of that night though, the Lord had moved upon those present in the most unexpected way. Several of the elderly congregation were slain in the Spirit, others began weeping and some were trembling and shaking under the power of God.

At another meeting the Lord started to touch the congregation during the message, before anyone could pray for them. People were even being slain in the Spirit while sitting in their seats; they were just slumped across their pews as the Spirit of God came upon them! Others, as I invited them forward for prayer, were going down under the power of God, and some of these were flat out on the floor for nearly an hour!

A sovereign outpouring of the Holy Spirit has been experienced right across this land, through the so called 'Toronto Blessing'. While this would seem to have been for a season, it certainly has not been without significance. During this time many thousands of Christians testified to a new dynamic relationship with the Lord. It re-envisioned God's people with a passion for Jesus; a greater burden for intercession gripped the Church; new worship songs and books on the work of the Holy Spirit were written and it brought a fresh urgency for evangelism. So much was accomplished in such an amazingly short time and I believe it was very much part of God's preparation for a revival that is yet to come.

The dynamic ministry of the Holy Spirit is something we need to embrace, that it might bring a greater measure of freedom into our lives and churches today. Streams of living water are flowing from the temple of God in the same way that it was spoken of in Ezekiel 47:1-12. There the prophet had a vision from the Lord of being led through water by degrees. At first the river came to his ankles, then to his knees and then to his waist.

Up to this point he was still firmly in control, but the next stage of the river was so deep that he could not continue walking. He was no longer able to move forward in his own strength, following his own direction; it was a river so deep that he had to swim. To make any further progress, Ezekiel needed to take his feet off the bottom and surrender himself to the flow and current of the river.

What a marvellous picture this is of God's purpose for every Christian. It speaks of a life completely yielded to the Lord's direction. Swimming in the living water of the Holy Spirit is the liberty God intends for us all; an experience where little effort is required, just the need to let go and relax in the flow of how the Spirit is moving. This is what God is bringing to the lives of Christians today, and until that liberty is found, then realising our full potential is not possible. We need to lose sight of ourselves and others, and be totally abandoned to God.

Nobody can adequately explain the experience of swimming to another who has never entered into water; they themselves have got to move in to find the freedom and enjoyment it brings. In the same way, with God's Spirit, a step of faith is required, particularly for those who have drawn a line in what they are prepared to accept saying, *"So far and no further."*

Those who allow their fears of possible excesses and who are unduly concerned about what is and is not of God, can find themselves missing what the Holy Spirit is doing. Some have prayed for years that they might see a visitation of the Holy Ghost, and then when the Lord begins to respond, their reaction is in effect, *"Lord we want you to bring revival, but we don't want it this way!"* The attitude of John Wesley, who was concerned about the dangers, but still wanting a move of God, is I believe helpful here. He prayed,

"O Lord send us the old revival, without the defects; but if this cannot be, send it with all its defects anyway. We must have revival!" He then went on to say, *"Be not alarmed that Satan sows tares among the wheat of Christ. It has ever been so, especially in any remarkable outpouring of the Holy Spirit; and ever will be until the devil is chained for a thousand years. Until then he will always ape, and endeavour to counteract the work of the Spirit of Christ."*

Let us have a look at some aspects of liberty in the Holy Spirit that help us to move on in our thinking. In doing so we will not only find a greater measure of freedom, but also see its relevance in fulfilling God's plan for our lives. Writing to the Church at Corinth, Paul said:

"When a man turns to the Lord the veil is removed. Now the Lord is the Spirit, and where the Spirit of the Lord is, there is freedom. And we all, with unveiled face, beholding

111

*the glory of the Lord, are being changed into His likeness
from one degree of glory to another; for this comes from the
Lord who is the Spirit."* (2 Corinthians 3:16-18).

Firstly, THE PLACE WHERE THIS LIBERTY IS FOUND

There is nothing wrong with travelling to a specific location and
seeking after God's anointing; in fact the effort and length we are
prepared to go to can express the sincerity of our heart towards God.
The truth of the matter is though, it is not primarily another country,
ministry, or church that is important. The grass always seems greener
elsewhere for certain Christians. Somewhere else always appears more
exciting and so we have people chasing all over, looking for the latest
'new thing' that God maybe doing. We don't have to get on a plane and
fly to Toronto, or Pensacola to find God's blessing. There is no need to
run after a man's ministry, or to go to another church so that we can
experience what He has for us. The place where liberty is found is
discovered in Paul's words,

*"**Where** the Spirit of the Lord is there is freedom."*

The key that unlocks the blessing of God into our lives is: where
God's Holy Spirit is present and welcomed; given room to work and
honoured; then there is God's provision of liberty.

Consider this principle first of all in the context of our individual
lives. This freedom can be experienced whether we are at home, at
work, in a traffic jam, or in the middle of a field. If we recognise God's
Spirit is with us and we honour His presence by the way we live, then
we will know liberty in any situation. This is demonstrated in the life of
the apostle John when he was exiled on the island of Patmos. In spite of
his predicament we see the freedom he had when he said, *"I was in the
Spirit on the Lord's Day...."* (Revelation 1:10). No amount of negative
circumstances need ever restrict the liberty we have in the Holy Spirit.

I recall being reminded of this during a frustrating occasion when
producing our quarterly newsletter. The photocopier we were using was
being very temperamental and this made our progress extremely slow.
Due to the fact that we had a deadline to meet I was coming under a

great deal of pressure and feeling quite stressed out. Then into my emotional turmoil God simply whispered, *"Where the Spirit of the Lord is there is freedom"*. As I started to dwell on these words and speak them out to myself, the revelation of their truth broke through. God reminded me that I didn't have to be under pressure; there was no need for me to be experiencing any stress, because His Holy Spirit was with me in that situation. Therefore, rather than getting all screwed up and tense inside, I started to rejoice and a freedom from the stress immediately came.

Because this work had taken so long, I was now running late for an appointment, so off I raced in my car. In heading towards the city centre, not only was the traffic very busy, all the cars appeared to be driving unnecessarily slowly and every traffic light seemed to change to red just as I came to it! As a result, again the feeling of pressure and stress was trying to grip my life. Into this situation God spoke to me once more saying, *"Where the Spirit of the Lord is there is freedom"*. When I began to believe and honour the truth that God's Spirit was not only with me in the car, but also the controlling influence of my life, I started to rejoice and give thanks. In taking my mind off the problem and setting my heart on God, all the anxiety and pressure lifted from me, and I got to my appointment on time!

The simple point is, we need to acknowledge God's Holy Spirit and welcome His presence in our lives, not just when we are within the four walls of a church building, but also in the daily circumstances we meet. God wants to set us free from the pressure of being caught up in the treadmill of activities, so that we acknowledge Him at all times.

In Romans 8:11 it says,
> *"If the Spirit of Him that raised up Jesus from the dead dwells in you, He that raised up Christ from the dead shall also quicken your mortal bodies by His Spirit that dwelleth in you."* (AV).

This is not just speaking about the resurrection we receive after death, it is something that happens right now also. We need a *"quickening"* that brings vitality to our mortal bodies, especially when pressures are weighing us down.

The principle we are speaking of is not only relevant in our individual experience, it is also appropriate for our corporate lives together. When we meet as believers, God's word says,

"For where two or three are gathered together in my name, there am I in the midst of them".

(Matthew 18:20, AV).

This is not merely the physical gathering of bodies together in a building, after all there are many church services that may be full, yet have little sense of freedom, or awareness of the Lord's presence among them. For His presence to be a reality that brings liberty, we have got to be together with one heart and mind; with one spirit and purpose. When we come like this, our focus is not on the congregation, or those leading the meeting, neither are we preoccupied with procedure and structure; instead our heart is on the Lord present amongst us, and as a result there is a glorious sense of freedom.

True unity and the recognition of the Lord among His people is a prominent characteristic in the book of Acts. When the believers first gathered together on the day of Pentecost we read,

"All these with one accord devoted themselves to prayer, together with the women...." (Acts 1:14).

Then again in Acts 4:32 it says,

"Now the company of those who believed were of one heart and soul, and no one said that any of the things which he possessed was his own, but they had everything in common."

The direct link between being together in unity and the blessing of God bringing liberty is seen in the words of David when he said,

"Behold, how good and pleasant it is when brothers dwell in unity!.... For there the Lord has commanded the blessing, ..."

(Psalm 133:1&3).

This is why miracles of release and blessing can be evident at every meeting, because the corporate joining together of Spirit-filled believers brings the presence of the Lord. Sometimes though, when we gather together, we come with all sorts of 'excess baggage.' We arrive with our doubts, fears, wrong attitudes and problems, then wonder why

114

there's a feeling of heaviness in the meeting and God's presence doesn't seem to be as real as it was. If, however, we come together as Spirit-filled believers, with faith in God, seeking His presence and acknowledging that He is the focal point, then the anointing that brings liberty begins to flow.

Secondly, THE PERSON WHO BRINGS THIS LIBERTY
The wonderful characteristic found as the Holy Spirit is poured out upon our lives is that the central figure is always the Lord. This is why God's word says, *"Where the Spirit of the Lord is there is freedom."*

What was so evident through the last visitation and refreshing that came upon the Church was that it clearly did not depend on man. God moved in a sovereign way and people were touched; sometimes through the laying on of hands and prayer, but more often than not, without any 'minister' doing anything.

The person, therefore, who brings this liberty is not a charismatic preacher, or even individuals giving testimony of an experience they have received somewhere else. These things may certainly help to build faith in others for what God is able to do, but our expectation must be in no-one other than the Lord. He will not share His glory with another. Too often man has tried to touch that glory and given the impression that it is through their ministry, or their abilities, that something is happening. We need to seek God and Him alone for what He wants to do. This takes a lot of pressure off the preacher and also the one leading the meeting because, in effect, they simply have to just step back and watch God minister!

Shortly before the Toronto blessing broke in this country back in 1994, several major national initiatives were organised to impact the community and inspire the Church. A lot of careful planning and preparation was involved and a great deal of expectation was raised in the hearts of thousands of Christians. Among these events were 'Jim Challenge', 'Minus to Plus' and 'On Fire'. While they were fruitful in their different ways, and we thank God for the lives that were affected through them, there was, however, a great deal of disappointment felt across the country by many. So much expense, expectation and effort had been put into these ventures and yet they had come to relatively little.

Then, following after this, came the extraordinary outpouring of God's Spirit throughout the United Kingdom and around the world, which took everyone by surprise. By early October 1994 it had touched an estimated 2,000 churches at least, and had ignited widespread debate both in the Christian and secular press. The mainstream media, including The Observer, The Independent, Daily Mail, The Times and The Daily Telegraph had all devoted large features to this phenomenon.

It was as though God was saying that we had planned, organised, and through our best efforts had tried our utmost, now He wanted us to stand still and watch what He was able to do, through a sovereign move of His Holy Spirit. This is something I believe we continually need reminding of so that we have a complete dependence on Him, rather than our own plans and strategies. David also points out the same thing when he says,

> ".... The Lord sets the prisoners free; the Lord opens the eyes of the blind. The Lord lifts up those who are bowed down; ...."
> (Psalm 146:7&8).

When talking about the liberty the Lord brings, we must also remember that when we come together it is to bow our knee to Jesus as Lord. We are not to come simply to be blessed, or refreshed as an end in itself, but to give our lives unreservedly to Him. It is in the giving of our lives that we receive the fullness of God's blessing. The scriptural principle is,

> "Give, and it will be given to you; good measure, pressed down, shaken together, running over, will be put into your lap. For the measure you give will be the measure you get back."
> (Luke 6:38).

Too many people come into a meeting with the wrong motive, but when we come to give ourselves in worship and service to God, then the power of His Spirit is poured out upon us. In surrendering our lives and turning to the Lord, the blessing of release and revelation comes.

We find this breakthrough spoken of in the passage we are considering in 2 Corinthians 3:16. Here it says,

*"When a man turns to the Lord **the veil is removed** .... "*

Notice God's word says that it is as we turn to Him the veil is removed. Sometimes Christians today, and many religious people, have a veil across their understanding. God seems distant; He doesn't appear to be relevant to their lives; they are unclear about His will; many just cannot see God's glory for themselves, and the freedom that they observe in others is dismissed as a carnal response of the flesh. When a person sincerely turns to the Lord, though, and their heart is diligently seeking after Him, then that which is obscuring their understanding is taken away.

This was the case for an elderly lady in Telford who responded for prayer. As the power of God came upon her she suddenly fell backwards right across some hard wooden chairs. Her fall was so heavy that I was extremely concerned she might have damaged herself. When I expressed this to her after the meeting she was surprised. Bubbling with excitement she told me that she hadn't felt a thing, and what was of greater interest to her was what happened while she was lying on the floor. She said, *"God has removed all the uncertainty I had in my mind and has shown me His plans for my future, and the ministry He has for my life!"*

Thirdly, THE PROVISION THIS LIBERTY PROMISES

There is freedom for everyone restricted, oppressed and held back in any way from being all that the Lord wants them to be. Some people are bound by their personality and don't realise it; they are inhibited and reserved by nature. One of the wonderful things that happened in the last outpouring of God's Spirit was the impact made on even the quietest, most reserved people. Those who looked the most respectable and undemonstrative came into a new liberty. Even these were rolling around the floor, hysterically laughing and shaking all over. The Spirit of the Lord moved upon people, and the British reserve that had been a great bondage in their lives was broken, bringing a new freedom.

In looking more closely, we discover that many other benefits become ours through the ministry of the Holy Spirit. These are:

(A) *Liberty In Praise And Worship*

The Scripture very relevant here is Psalm 16:11, *".... in thy presence there is fullness of joy..."* One of the evidences of the presence of God in a meeting, or in our lives, is "fullness of joy". Notice that we aren't talking simply about happiness and a feeling of well being, nor even just joy, but "fullness of joy"! This experience is evident throughout Church history in every revival, and is something that the Bible speaks about in the city of Samaria, where the Spirit of the Lord was touching lives. The impact God's presence made on others as they were saved, healed, delivered and filled with the Spirit was so great that the scripture says, *"There was much joy in that city."* (Acts 8:8).

It isn't stretching the imagination too much, therefore, to suggest that this amount of joy must involve a lot of emotion, include a great deal of noise, require much celebration and result in considerable laughter. Fullness of joy suggests an exuberance and an extravagance in our worship.

The freedom we have in worship is very relative. We can think we have liberty, but then we visit another church and experience the freedom they have, and we realise we are still restricted. Occasionally I have the privilege of ministering in black Pentecostal Churches, and these people worship God with a freedom that I've never found anywhere else. They know a liberty in the Holy Spirit that I believe challenges our so-called freedom.

When we are talking about a response to God that is an intimate, personal response of love, we can only learn so much from books, tapes and videos. It is something that you cannot adequately teach people. There needs to come a move of God upon that person's life to set them free to worship Him. The Spirit of the Lord, therefore, releases us to know a joyful exuberance that is not inhibited by the opinions and criticism of others.

There will always be those who are quick to offer their opinions, criticising another's liberty, and it is interesting to note that almost always this disapproval will come from the religious. When you start to get free and are enthusiastic in your response to the Lord, then the religious get stirred up to oppose, labelling you a fanatic!

This has always been the case, and an example is found in the account of Jesus' entry into Jerusalem, in Luke 19:37-40. Here we read,
"The whole multitude of disciples began to rejoice and praise God with a loud voice."
Their response to the presence of the Lord was not orchestrated or rehearsed, it was spontaneous and the reaction of the Pharisees was to immediately scorn the extravagance of their emotion. They wanted Jesus to make them be quiet so they said,
"Teacher, rebuke your disciples". (verse 39b).
When we hear the Lord's reply to their criticism we learn that He expected such a response, in fact He thought it completely normal. Jesus said,
"I tell you, if these were silent, the very stones would cry out." (verse 40).

Also, on the day of Pentecost, when the Holy Spirit was poured out on the believers they began praising God with such enthusiasm that others mocked, saying they were drunk! Peter's response to this was,
"For these men are not drunk, as you suppose, since it is only the third hour of the day; ...." (Acts 2:15).
The reason those mocking had come to such a strange conclusion was because the disciples were acting like drunken men. They had no inhibitions or self-consciousness; rather, being full of the Holy Spirit, they were liberated from themselves to worship God.

(B) *Liberty From Lukewarm Living*
When apathy and complacency creeps into our Christian experience we are in a very dangerous position. God shows His hatred to such a lukewarm relationship in the strong rebuke He gave to the Christian church at Laodicea. He said,

"So, because you are lukewarm, and neither cold nor hot,
I will spew you out of my mouth."　　　　(Revelation 3:16).

It is usually by degrees that we lose our fervour and become complacent. I was reminded of this in reading an article recently from the devotional booklet, Daily Bread, about the danger of spiritual decline. Apparently, observers have learned that a frog is vulnerable if placed in a pan of water that is slowly being heated. Since the body temperature of this little cold-blooded creature changes to correspond with its surroundings, he is unaware of the danger. Before the frog realises it, he is in boiling-hot water, and death overtakes him. This, for ourselves as Christians, is why we need to daily acknowledge our dependence on the Holy Spirit. It's the only way to avoid a cold heart that gets us into hot water!

The Spirit of the Lord firstly brings conviction, then release, and a refreshing to stir us up again with an enthusiasm in our hearts as we serve the Lord. Peter refers to this in Acts 3:19 when he says,
"Repent therefore, and turn again, that your sins may be
blotted out, that times of refreshing might come from the
presence of the Lord."
When we come to the place of a right relationship with God and we ask His forgiveness for the things we have allowed to affect our love, then His Holy Spirit brings a refreshing.

New motivation comes into our lives that fires us up in everything we are involved with. This is important, because all we do as Christians is done either out of duty, or out of desire. Whether we are attending meetings, praying, teaching in the Sunday School, playing a musical instrument, giving out the hymn books, operating the overhead projector, or giving in the offering etc., we either do these things because we want to, or because we feel we ought to. In everything that is done, God's instruction is that we,
"Serve the Lord with gladness!"　　　　(Psalm 100:2a).
The only way we can keep a glad and willing heart is through the refreshing power of the Holy Spirit, that liberates us from ever feeling that what we are doing is a heavy burden.

120

Paul, when speaking about this motivation, said,

"Never flag in zeal, be aglow with the Spirit, serve the Lord." (Romans 12:11).

Let us not settle for being merely a 'sunbeam for Jesus,' rather let us not be satisfied with anything less than being a 'blazing torch' for the Lord, so that we live with all our might until the flame goes out!

(C) *Liberty From the Defeat Of Temptation*

Those weak, vulnerable areas of our lives that cause us to fail, and the habitual sins which bring a sense of frustration and condemnation, can be conquered. By the power and presence of the Holy Spirit we can not only be set free, but also strengthened to remain free.

As a boy, the well known Bible teacher F. B. Meyer enjoyed visiting the science building of a Polytechnic in London. One of the exhibits he liked most was a diving bell. It had no bottom, but there were seats attached to the rim at its base. At various times throughout the day, visitors were allowed to enter the diving bell and occupy those seats. It was then lowered into a deep tank of water. What fascinated Meyer was the fact that no water ever came up into the bell, even though its occupants could have reached out and dipped their fingers in.

The reason it didn't fill with water is that air was constantly being pumped into the bell from above. If a vacuum had existed, water would have rushed in. F. B. Meyer then made this application to believers:

"If you are full of the Holy Ghost the flesh life is underneath you, and although it would surge up, it is kept out."

When we let the Lord by His Holy Spirit fill and control the inner man, then the world with all its pressures cannot control the outer man. The provision of the Holy Spirit and His purpose at work within our lives was always what the apostle Paul depended on, and something he felt very important for others. His prayer for the Ephesian Christians was,

".... according to the riches of His glory may He grant you to be strengthened with might through His Spirit in the inner man." (Ephesians 3:16).

There is a promise given to us in God's word that is guaranteed to make a dramatic difference in the area of being free from the defeat of temptation. It is direct and to the point and says,

"Live by the Spirit, and you will not gratify the desires of the sinful nature." (Galatians 5:16, NIV).

When our lives are governed by the Spirit of the Lord there is liberty from the dominant power of sin and the defeat it brings.

(D) *Liberty From Physical Sickness*

The Lord is still a miracle-working, life-changing, need-meeting God. He has not changed! The bondage that sickness brings us into and the restriction it places on us is something that God's presence has greater power over. We read of this in Luke 5:17:

".... and the power of the Lord was present to heal them."

Throughout the ministry of Jesus this was always the case. Wherever He was present then miracles happened, and our confidence should be the same today. His power has not diminished in any way, we just have to honour the truth that, *"Where the Spirit of the Lord is there is freedom"* and put our faith in it unconditionally.

Over the years it has been wonderful to pray for thousands of people in the area of healing and see the Lord work many miracles in their lives. One of the most memorable occasions that I'll never forget though, was a remarkable healing I experienced myself.

The day before travelling away in ministry, I managed somehow to strain my back whilst playing with my daughters. This was hardly noticeable at the time, but the following day, as I travelled up to Manchester, it was starting to ache slightly. Having preached at the meeting that evening, I returned with my hosts to their house for the night. By now my back was becoming more painful, but not to any great degree. On waking the next morning though, it became apparent that something was seriously wrong. I couldn't move at all without being in agony. My hosts, thinking that I was having a lie-in, had both gone to work, so I was left alone and didn't know their telephone number.

122

There was nothing I could do about the situation so I just lay there for several hours. Eventually I decided to try and get up, because I had a meeting to take that night in Rochdale. As I attempted to move, a sharp, unbearable pain shot up and down my spine. In spite of this, somehow I managed to inch my way out of bed and down on to the floor. Very slowly I crawled along, but at every movement there was intense pain. Several more hours passed, and by this time I'd only reached the bedroom door. I now had the stairs to navigate so I could get down to the lounge and phone a doctor.

Eventually, after six hours on the floor, I achieved this and, when the doctor arrived, he examined me carefully and said that I'd pulled the muscles in my back badly and would need complete rest for a week. It was at this point I reluctantly rang the Pastor of the church in Rochdale to explain that my visit would have to be cancelled. On putting down the phone and feeling quite despondent I continued to lie flat on the floor. While doing this I remembered the scripture, *"Where the Spirit of the Lord is there is freedom."*

At first I gave no further thought to it, but as the words kept coming to me, the revelation of their truth broke through. Jesus my healer was with me in that room; the one who could bring deliverance from my physical bondage was beside me! It was then that I began to praise God and ask for His healing power to bring release.

Having prayed this I thought that I'd better get up, and that's exactly what I did. Twenty minutes after seeing the doctor I went back upstairs, got dressed, packed and loaded my luggage into the car, then drove off to speak at Rochdale. Not only did the Lord enable me to speak at this meeting, but also to finish the rest of my itinerary without any problem at all.

No-one would have any difficulty believing for their healing if the Lord stood in His literal physical presence before them. In fact, there would most likely be a frantic scramble of people with needs surging forward if that was the case. Why is it, therefore, that the same level of faith is very often absent when the opportunity for prayer is given to people here in this country?

During my time in Africa it was an inspiration to see the simple faith of Christians there, and in the crusade meetings many outstanding miracles of healing took place. This happened, I believe, because when we preached that Jesus was present and wanted to heal the sick, they took the good news at face value and just came to receive. When our confidence is in the promise of God's word, rather than the ministry of man, the assurance we have is,

> *"Many are the afflictions of the righteous; but the Lord delivers him out of all of them."* (Psalm 34:19).

(E) *Liberty From Emotional Struggles*

One good definition of emotional wholeness is, "To be at peace with our past, our present and our future". It surely is self-evident that when we are not, this can restrict us from realising our full potential.

When Jesus stood up in the synagogue and declared, *"The Spirit of the Lord is upon me..."* one of the purposes for that anointing He said would be, *"to set at liberty those who are oppressed"*. (Luke 4:18). Jesus came to heal the wounded spirit; helping those who had been crushed by cruel blows to be free from the effect of rejection, fear, discouragement, disappointment, frustration etc. This liberty from every negative influence in our emotions was expressed by the Psalmist when he spoke of his own experience saying,

> *"Thou hast turned for me my mourning into dancing;....."*
> (Psalm 30:11).

The Lord brings freedom from the many things that cause sadness and oppression to people. In the recent visitation of His Holy Spirit, it was wonderful to see how heaviness was miraculously turned into joy. God brought the incredible phenomena of laughter to His Church, and lives were never the same again. When this happened, what occurred in many cases was that all the tensions, hurts and bottled-up emotions which had oppressed people were released. The things that had overshadowed lives and had grown out of all proportion were being dealt with and their hold over people was broken.

Those who had not been able to laugh for a long time were released, as the healing power of the Lord came into their emotions. It

124

is a proven fact, according to the 'experts,' that laughter does have a healing effect, both physically and emotionally. Here we see the wisdom of God revealed in His ministry to us. The Bible says,

"*A cheerful heart is a good medicine ....*" (Proverbs 17:22).

The experts are only now proving what we have always known, and they are agreeing with God!

I recall vividly an incident at the end of a meeting in Co. Durham when an unusual stillness came upon the congregation, and then unexpectedly a wave of laughter swept over everyone in the building. This was unprompted by anyone, and became uncontrollable as people were staggering about full of joy. Among those there that were helped, were several who shared with me about the deep hurts and fears they had carried for many years? Also, some spoke of the effect that past sexual abuse had had in their lives, causing depression, and others referred to demonic oppression that had brought torment to them.

When people enter into God's provision of restoration from all that the enemy has stolen from them, and they see their full inheritance in Christ, it's not surprising that they should express that joy in laughter. We see how scriptural this is in Psalm 126:1&2. Here David says,

"*When the Lord restored the fortunes of Zion, we were like those who dream. Then our mouth was filled with laughter, and our tongue with shouts of joy ....*"

LOOKING BEYOND OURSELVES

The most important aspect of any new experience of liberty in the Holy Spirit, is how it impacts our lives to more fervently love and live for God. If we overlook this, then we have missed the whole point of His grace and mercy in visitation. The purpose of liberty in the Holy Spirit is not simply that we might be rolling around the floor in uncontrollable laughter, or that we might settle down with a wonderful experience. It is that we might be transformed into the likeness of Jesus.

Paul refers to this in 2 Corinthians 3:18 when he says,

*"And we all, with unveiled face, beholding the glory of the Lord, are being **changed into His likeness** from one degree of glory unto another; for this comes from the Lord who is the Spirit."*

The mistake so easily made in something like the Toronto blessing, is that this new liberty becomes an excuse for indulgence and self-satisfaction. Wonderful though it is to be blessed, refreshed, released and renewed, we can't stay on the 'mountain top' indefinitely. Some people are just like Peter on the mount of transfiguration. They become so taken up with the experience of the moment that they forget there is a world full of need beneath them in the valley.

God brings His power and presence into our lives that we might be changed to be like Jesus, particularly in passion and purpose. The experience of God's Holy Spirit is intended to make us more effective in presenting Him to the world. This is the evidence of a Spirit-filled life, and is the expression of any genuine encounter with God.

It is not so important, therefore, how a person goes down under the power of the Holy Spirit, but how they get up again, that is what really counts.

The Prayer of Charles H. Spurgeon, who was Pastor of the Metropolitan Tabernacle in London, should stir us all to rise up with a new passion that sees beyond our own personal blessing. He said,

"O God, send us a season of glorious disorder; O for a sweep of the wind that will set the seas in motion and make our iron-clad brethren, lying so deep in anchor, to roll from stern to stern. O for the fire to fall again, fire that shall affect the most solid. O that such fire, that first sat upon the disciples, might fall on all around. Thou art ready to work with us today, even as thou did then. Stay not we beseech thee, but work at once. Break down every barrier that hinders the incoming of your might. Give us now both hearts of flame and tongues of fire to preach thy reconciling word, for Jesus' sake, Amen."

God wants each of us to know a greater liberty in the Holy Spirit individually and corporately in our churches. This liberty though, is not an end in itself, but is given that we might realise our full potential of being like Christ. We must keep the focus of our faith upon Jesus and seek after Him rather than an experience. As we surrender our lives to the Lord, the freedom He leads us into will bring a priority and passion for the lost, so that we can, as we shall see in the next chapter, walk in the power of God.

Chapter 8

Walking In The Power Of God

A young police recruit was set a problem to answer in a training exam that proved rather a challenge to him. The question read:

'While on the beat you see two dogs fighting. They knock a baby out of its pram which causes a car to swerve off the road and smash into a grocer's shop. This results in a pedestrian being injured. During the confusion a woman's bag is snatched. The crowd of onlooker's chase after the thief and, in the huge build up of traffic, the ambulance is blocked from getting through to the victim of the crash. State, in order of priority, your course of action.'

His answer was: *"Take off uniform and mingle with the crowd!"*

Amusing as this may sound, sometimes the Church responds in much the same way to the urgent needs in society today? Getting involved in the problems of life is the responsibility of every Christian and part of God's call upon our lives. Rather than *'mingling with the crowd'* we ought to be stepping forward, meeting every need with the practical love and power of the gospel.

The attitude expressed by William Booth, founder of the Salvation Army, is a considerable contrast to that of the inexperienced police recruit, and an example to us all. He said:

"While women weep, as they do now, I'll fight; while children go hungry, as they do now I'll fight; while men go to prison, in and out, in and out, as they do now, I'll fight; while there is a drunkard left, while there is a poor lost girl upon the streets, while there remains one dark soul without the light of God, I'll fight; - I'll fight to the very end!"

This is a passion that must be inspired by the Holy Spirit, otherwise, in our zeal we will be sharing the good news of God's love in our own strength. The Lord wants us to walk under His anointing, but to do so, we must see that walking in the power of God is totally inseparable from witnessing to the people around us. It is because the Church has overlooked this for so long that the evidence of God's power has often been absent in its activities.

The instructions given by Jesus to His disciples could not have been made clearer. Having told them to wait in Jerusalem for the necessary anointing from heaven, Jesus then says,
"You shall receive power when the Holy Spirit has come upon you; and you shall be my witnesses...."   (Acts 1:8).

These two aspects of truth, *"You shall receive...* and, *You shall be..."* are intended to be one, just as they were for the early Church. They experienced multitudes being converted and saw outstanding healings and deliverances because they recognised that the provision of power was for the purpose of witnessing. Once you separate one aspect of God's word from the other you render the truth ineffective and powerless. Due to the problem of this 'great divorce' today, God is stirring His Church that it might return to New Testament living.

Sometimes we can be tempted to accept complacency and apathy as normal; as though it is something we just have to live with. Because of this, it is at times difficult to see the Church ever having a significant voice in society as at one time it did.

Also, we tend to be very small-minded in this country. Most Christians would consider that they were part of a large church if the membership were perhaps two hundred. In other nations of the world though, like Brazil, Argentina, Chile, China, Colombia, South Korea etc., the congregations are enormous! Where the Holy Spirit is being poured out we find phenomenal church growth, and a noticeable impact on the community.

God is, I believe, preparing us for a breakthrough in our own nation and, because of this, we have to lift our expectation for bigger and greater things to happen in us, so that we walk in His power. As the Lord pours out His Holy Spirit upon the Church, He brings a greater awareness of Himself and what He is able to do. This is important because what will ignite the dryness of religion, and spread the flames of revival, is a revelation of the pre-eminence of Christ, and faith that rests in the unchanging power of God.

THE PRE-EMINENCE OF CHRIST

Christianity is not so much a religion as a revelation; one that is based on the power of God to exalt the Lord Jesus Christ. Jesus triumphed over sin, bringing righteousness, conquered hatred, bringing love, and He overcame Satan's oppression and hold on people, bringing a glorious freedom. Our emphasis therefore, must never get distracted from the centrality of Christ, and the importance of the gospel to our daily lives. This is why the Bible says,

"He is the head of the body, the church; He is the beginning, the first-born from the dead, that in everything He might be pre-eminent." (Colossians 1:18).

Very often when people read this verse they only think about it in a religious context. They consider it refers to religious activities like prayer, worship, preaching, church programmes, planning etc. This phrase, *"in everything"*, is extremely important because it reminds us that in all aspects of our life, including our marriage, family, working life, leisure activities, motives, priorities etc., in everything Christ should have the first place of prominence. If we are to know God's power in our lives He must be the centre of everything.

Unfortunately, there are churches that give little expression to the centrality of Christ in their daily affairs. Some have grown introvert and, although they have a high regard for the scriptures, there is little contact or relevance to the community of which they are a part. Others are so busy sorting out various tensions and disagreements among themselves that they have lost sight of those outside their circle. Their focus isn't on Jesus, it's on problems.

Then there are other churches that have a strong emphasis on social action, but lack any mention of repentance and a person's need to get right with God. This results in them presenting only a social gospel and Jesus gets marginalised. He is no longer the centre and substance of the message, but is pushed out to the fringe.

With certain churches, especially some Pentecostal, House Church, and Charismatic groups, they get side-tracked on to a particular aspect of doctrine and this becomes their main emphasis. We have a wide variety to listen to today, such as those who preach the gospel of healing, the gospel of prosperity, the gospel of deliverance, and the 'Faith Gospel.' All these are important aspects of truth, but once you major on one particular thing, to the exclusion of the whole, you become unbalanced and pre-occupied with a doctrine, rather than Christ. People then get taken up with an aspect of truth, rather than *the* truth Himself.

Paul was very concerned about this danger. He not only wanted his own life to be balanced, but also every church he visited to be balanced as well. He considered there were two important things that would achieve this in people's lives. Paul speaks of them in 1 Corinthians 2:1-5. Here, in addressing a very unbalanced and carnal congregation, he says,

"When I came to you, brethren, I did not come proclaiming to you the testimony of God in lofty words or wisdom. For I decided to know nothing among you except Jesus Christ and Him crucified. And I was with you in weakness and in much fear and trembling; and my speech and my message were not in plausible words of wisdom, but in demonstration of the Spirit and of power, that your faith might not rest in the wisdom of men but in the power of God."

The apostle, of course, believed in deliverance and he taught prosperity. He was convinced about the necessity of faith and was committed to the good news of healing. All these aspects of truth he preached clearly and practised actively. However, the first passion and priority of his life was expressed in his determination to know nothing among them except, *"Jesus Christ and Him crucified."* Uppermost in all his thoughts was the pre-eminence of Jesus.

Paul understood, however, that this alone was not sufficient to bring balance. What he realised to be of equal importance was that people's faith might, *"rest in the power of God"*. He believed these two great truths were both part of the gospel, and that one without the other was incomplete.

GOD'S UNCHANGING POWER

Right at the heart of the Christian faith is the revelation that God's power in Christ is the same today as it was 2,000 years ago. This is why the Bible says,

> *"Jesus Christ is the same yesterday and today and*
> *forever."* (Hebrews 13:8).

He is the same friend of sinners, healer of sickness, baptiser in the Holy Spirit and the same mighty deliverer. Jesus remains the same, unlike our British weather, modern fashion, popular music, or the moods of people. The Lord is: constant in His love, reliable in His promises, firm in His faithfulness, and unchanging in His power!

The one key verse that unlocks our ability to walk in a greater measure of God's power is found in the words of Paul when, with deep conviction he said,

> *"For I am not ashamed of the gospel: it is the power of*
> *God for salvation to every one who has faith ... "* (Romans 1:16).

As we consider this scripture it shows us three things that must be in our lives if we are to fulfil our full potential.

Firstly, A POSITIVE IDENTIFICATION

We need to unashamedly be identified with the good news of Jesus. Paul could say, *"I am not ashamed of the gospel ..... "* We should be able to put our name in this verse and see ourselves standing with the same commitment. Rather than being reluctant, passive or indifferent about the gospel, we ought to be glad and enthusiastic to be identified with Christ. Unlike the person who, in a church service when the preacher asked, *"Can everyone hear me at the back?"*, replied from the far corner of the hall, *"Yes, but I wouldn't mind changing places with someone who can't!"*

Now, as never before, is the time for us to stand up and be counted, to raise our voice and speak out in a positive way about the gospel? There is no need for us to apologise to others about what we believe, or feel embarrassed about Jesus, neither should we be intimidated by the attitude of the majority. For far too long the Church in this nation, which should have a prophetic voice in society, has remained strangely quiet, but God is calling us to speak out.

WE CAN MAKE A DIFFERENCE

A tiny minority of people can make a huge impact upon the majority, if only they will stand for what they believe and have the courage of their convictions. Minority groups today like the Gay Movement, people concerned about animal rights, and those who are outspoken about the environment, all have a significant effect upon the thinking and attitudes of the majority.

The commitment of these people toward what they believe is a challenge to the Christian Church in these days. The Gay Movement is a case in point. We can be completely deceived by the media and those in this pressure group, as to the actual size of the homosexual community in our country. What we are talking about is a tiny percentage of the total population, yet they have a far reaching influence upon the standards of the majority, even changing legislation in our land. Their values are gradually replacing the righteous standard of God's word, and as a result, the moral fabric of society is crumbling.

The reason why such a small group can influence the masses is because they stand up, speak out and protest, until slowly, little by little, their cause is not only listened to, but progressively accepted as normal. Meanwhile, the Church stands triumphantly by saying, *"I am not ashamed of the gospel."*

Again, when you look at those who are so devoted and passionate about 'green issues' and protecting the environment, the same influence

134

is exerted by the minority over the majority. In the early days of their cause few people listened to them. They seemed to have a lone voice and were disregarded by many as somewhat eccentric. Today, however, many respect their concerns and adopt some of their views, if not always agreeing with their methods.

A few years ago, while travelling towards Leytonstone in London, I drove past part of Epping Forest where a large protest meeting was being held. Police in protective clothing were everywhere and the press, radio and television were also assembled. Security guards were chasing after protestors, workmen were running around with chain-saws and up in the trees, from branch to branch, nets were strewn all over. Some of the protesters had even made homes in the trees and had spent several nights in uncomfortable and precarious circumstances.

All this commotion and concern was taking place because they were wanting to save the trees! What incredible commitment and sacrifice, and the Church sits down whispering, *"I am not ashamed of the gospel."*

Also, when we think about those who get so worked up about animal rights, again the same level of emotion and degree of commitment is seen.

Having preached at Margate in Kent on one occasion, I travelled the following day across to Ramsgate and as I came to the area of the docks a huge crowd was gathered. Police were there in great numbers, keeping a watchful eye, and the press also was present. Among those in the crowd were people as young as six and others as old as ninety! They had been standing, reasonably quietly, for hours, equipped with banners, posters and placards. Then as soon as they caught sight of the cattle-lorries arriving, they erupted into a furious rage. All of them began to shout out in protest about the rights of the cattle being exported. They stamped their feet, waved their fists and screamed as loud as they were able.

All this was because ordinary people, of all ages, from every walk of life, wanted to save the cattle. And the Church walks silently away thinking, *"I am not ashamed of the gospel"*.

Today we are living at a time when people want to save the whales, save the seals and save the ozone layer, but God has called you and I to save men and women! The only thing that can save people from the bondage of Satan and the prospect of a lost eternity, is the message and power of the gospel.

It is not sufficient, though, for there merely to be just an identification with the gospel. If we are going to influence others for Christ, in any meaningful way, then there needs to be a *positive* identification. For this to be the case we must:

(A) *Re-Capture The Joy Of The Gospel*

The gospel is good news! The greatest message this world could ever hear, but unless it stirs, thrills and excites our hearts, it will never make any difference to others. We may well try to articulate the message as we speak to someone about Jesus, but unless it burns within us, and we are convinced of its good news, then it will leave others untouched and completely cold.

If we compared the greatest news we could receive personally with how we feel about the gospel, it would give an indication as to how much the message we've been entrusted with really means. The birth of a child for example, or maybe coming into a large inheritance, perhaps some promotion at work, or the news of passing our driving test. All these things are wonderful and certainly well able to move our emotions, but shouldn't the gospel equally, not only inform our minds, but also stir our hearts, putting a fire within us that the flood of opposition could never put out?

This was the experience of Peter and John. Their positive identification with the gospel is seen when they were threatened and told never to speak about Jesus again. Peter's reaction to these threats is to say,

".... We cannot but speak of what we have seen and heard."
(Acts 4:20).
Jeremiah also, when referring to the emotion he felt concerning God's word, said,
"Thy word is like a burning fire shut up in my bones".
(Jeremiah 20:9).
This is a very real experience. It is not something we can pretend we have, or work up ourselves; we've either got it or we haven't. If we are to know greater effectiveness in influencing others for Christ though, then we must re-capture the joy and excitement of the gospel.

(B) *Re-evaluate Our Priorities In Relation To The Gospel*

The gospel is not something we merely go to church to hear; it is something we go from church to tell. We must ask ourselves, do we live and breathe to see people won to Christ? Those in the New Testament Church did. It is no wonder that these people walked in the power of God and saw such amazing results. Their number one priority was to make Jesus known everywhere they went, to whoever they could. They weren't fulfilling their religious obligation, they really wanted to witness to others.

The great evangelist George Whitefield once said, *"God forbid that I should travel with anybody a quarter of an hour without speaking of Christ to them."*

How high on our personal agenda does this priority really come? Sometimes making Christ known to others is far from being foremost in our thinking, planning, praying and speaking. It is true that only God can bring salvation to people, and no-one but the Holy Spirit can cause conviction, but you and I are the ones the Lord has entrusted to sow the seed of the His gospel.

Over forty years ago the well known missionary to China, Hudson Taylor, cried out, *"I cannot go on living unless I tell the people of China about Jesus".*

He personally trained a thousand missionaries, an army of native workers, and planted the Church in that nation. Today it is a hundred million strong and growing! The example of such people is well worth reflecting upon, then asking ourselves the question, *"Do I have a burden for the lost, or have I lost the burden?"*

(C) *Re-discover Our Confidence In The Gospel*

Some people, because of their shyness and introvert nature, say that involvement in evangelism isn't their ministry. As a result they don't even attempt to share their faith. It certainly is right that not everyone is an evangelist, but we are all called to be Christ's witnesses. If we are to be everything God has purposed us to be, we must re-discover our confidence, so that we can speak of Jesus fearlessly, without feeling odd, awkward, nervous, or inadequate.

When we look at the believers in the New Testament we find they had a holy boldness that was nothing to do with their personality. They had been equipped by the Holy Spirit to do the work of God, and it was from their relationship with the Lord that they were given the confidence to stand and make known the gospel. In Acts 4:13 it says,

> *"Now when they saw the boldness of Peter and John, and perceived that they were uneducated, common men, they wondered; and they recognised that they had been with Jesus."*

We see from this incident that our confidence communicates Christ. It always has and always will. Whilst this is true, we find also that our confidence will get us into trouble as well. When a person begins to stand up and speak out for Jesus they will 'stir up a hornet's nest'. Alarming as at first this might sound, it is one of the marks of leading a godly life.

According to the Bible, godliness isn't seen merely in that we speak in tongues, have liberty to dance in worship, or shout loudly in prayer. It is that we cause a reaction in others by our commitment to Christ. Paul mentioned this when writing to his young disciple Timothy. He said,

> *"Indeed all who desire to live a godly life in Christ Jesus will be persecuted."* (2 Timothy 3:12).

138

We certainly don't go looking for trouble, but it will soon find us when we begin to speak out for the Lord!

Some people will be upset, but others saved as we witness about Jesus. This is what the disciples experienced because of their radical commitment. In this politically correct age in which we live, where so much concern is shown to accommodate all beliefs, we need to be radical also. That takes courage and is only possible when our confidence is in the Lord.

Secondly, A PRESENT REALISATION

Paul said concerning the gospel, *" ... . it is the power of God for salvation"*. Our confidence comes from the fact that not only do we believe the gospel is true, we also know that it works too. Change in people's lives is not brought about through philosophy, psychology, religiosity, methodology, nor even theology. What makes the difference is a present realisation of the gospel's power in a person's life. Not just that it was historically 2,000 years ago, or that it will be hopefully sometime in the future when revival comes. The truth that must be grasped is that right here and now the gospel **is** the power of God.

What will also make a significant difference to us, especially in circumstances of difficulty, is realising, *"the gospel is the power of God for salvation"*. This word salvation is wonderful because it doesn't just speak about when we first come to Christ for forgiveness and are saved from a lost eternity; it also affects our lives today. I was 'saved' over 27 years ago, but I am being saved every single day. The salvation of God is needed in our lives right now!

It is the only answer to our present situation; God's response to meet our immediate needs. Salvation lifts the burden, brings back the joy, sustains us through times of trial, strengthens us to overcome, heals us in our sickness, rescues us from the hand of the evil one, and so much more. God's salvation is His provision of wholeness, to meet our every need, at all times, wherever we are.

The gospel is still, today, the power of God to change lives, impact cities, and to destroy the works of the devil.

(A) *The Power of God To Change Lives*

No-one knew the truth of this more than the apostle Paul. It's not surprising therefore, that he could speak about the gospel with such conviction. He was changed from being a murderer to a missionary; transformed from a Christ hater to a Christ proclaimer. Paul knew from personal experience its life changing power.

As we think of this, we are reminded that the gospel is God's power to change the lives of even those people who are not seeking after Christ. Before Paul's conversion he was not seeking after Jesus with any intention of worshipping Him; far from it. He wanted to wipe out any mention of Christ. This is particularly encouraging when we think of the friends and loved ones we have who are showing no interest in the gospel, particularly those who are hostile. Sometimes we can be tempted to give up on such people ever being saved.

While looking through the 'Word For Today' devotional booklet by U.C.B., I read the extraordinary testimony of God's power to change the life of a man who seemed beyond hope. This is what it said:

'If God could redeem Billy Elliott, the leader of one of Northern Ireland's para-military organisations, then there's hope for anybody. One morning Billy's brother-in-law borrowed his car to take his daughter to school. But when he turned on the ignition and backed out of the driveway, the car exploded into a fireball and killed him instantly. That was only one of the many attempts his enemies made on his life.

Gradually the idealism of Billy's youth turned to disillusionment. One night as he lay in the Maze prison in Belfast, tears filled his eyes as he remembered a childhood song, *"Jesus loves me this I know, for the Bible tells me so"*. He wondered, *"God, could you ever forgive a man like me?"* Soon after he received the answer.

When he got out of prison, he went to hear Dr James McConnell preaching about King David. He said, *"In spite of adultery and murder God forgave him and He can do it for you too"*. That night Billy Elliot took the broken pieces of his life and gave them to Jesus. Seven years later, he is in the ministry. Today he goes into the fields where he once trained his men in territorial warfare, sets up big gospel tents, then goes and brings them to hear about Jesus. This past summer, more than 600 of them came to Christ. Recently, in New Jersey, he shared his testimony with leaders from 150 nations.'

Another encouraging reminder, for myself, of God's power to change lives, was a pastor's daughter that I met while preaching at Warrington a few years ago. Just before the meeting this woman, who was 24 years old, shared her testimony with me. Throughout most of her teenage years she had fallen away from God and was in rebellion to His will for her life. Although she was a Christian, she'd come to the point of deciding to turn her back on Christianity and go her own way.

This continued for several years, until one night late in her teens, she was driving home from work when she noticed a large poster on a bus shelter, across the road from where she lived. It was advertising one of the Disney films, 'The Lion King'. What caught her attention was the message on the poster. In large bold black letters she read the words, **"THE KING IS COMING!"**

This immediately convicted her and, right there in the car, she broke down and wept uncontrollably as she was reminded that Jesus the King was coming, and she wasn't ready!

That woman is now on fire for the Lord and totally committed to God's work, in fact she's leading the youth group in her church. Later this year she is getting married to a fine Christian man who she met shortly after re-committing her life to Jesus.

Isn't God wonderful! What she saw wasn't a scripture verse, or some religious poster, but it's marvellous the way God is able to use anything to confront people and change their lives by the power of His gospel.

(B) *The Power of God To Impact Cities*

William Wilberforce was a great Christian philanthropist and vigorous opponent of the slave trade in England during the early 1800's. As he surveyed the terrible moral and spiritual climate of his day, he did not lose hope, but had faith in the power of the gospel to bring change. He wrote,

> *"My own solid hopes for the well-being of my country depend not so much on her navies or armies, nor on the wisdom of her rulers, nor on the spirit of her people, as on the persuasion that she still contains many who love and obey the gospel of Christ. I believe that their prayers may yet prevail."*

Within a few years after he made this statement, the country he loved experienced one of the greatest revivals in modern times, bringing salvation to thousands and producing widespread social changes.

When we think of what would be necessary to make an impact on our community or town, we might well consider the importance of a clearly defined strategy and army of trained personnel. Modern technology and sophisticated communications would be helpful as well. The Bible, however, shows us that God's ways are certainly not our ways. When we read about the impact made by the disciples, we discover that all they needed was confidence in the power of the gospel.

In Acts 8 revival is taking place and the whole community is affected. Verse 5 says,

> *"Philip went down to a city of Samaria, and proclaimed to them the Christ. And the multitudes with one accord gave heed to what was said by Philip, when they heard him and saw the signs which he did. For unclean spirits came out of many who were possessed, crying with a loud voice; and many who were paralysed or lame were healed .... ."*

What we find here is one man, with one message, who had faith in one Almighty God! Philip walked in the power of God, speaking under the anointing of the Holy Spirit, and lives were changed. When he preached the gospel, he expected something to happen. This is the tragedy in our churches today; we don't expect anything to happen when the gospel is presented. Indeed, some people would get the shock of their lives if, when they spoke to another about Christ, that person immediately turned round and asked, *"What have I got to do to be saved?"*

The place we must come back to today, in the Church, is where we expect God to confirm His word with signs and wonders. It is because of disappointment and discouragement that we have allowed the enemy to slowly erode this anticipation, to the extent that we don't really expect much to happen.

We ought to be encouraged that the seeds of revival throughout the region of Samaria were sown by the most unlikely person. In John 4 we find that it was an immoral woman, whose heart was far from God, that the Lord used. She meets Jesus at a well and when He asks where her husband is, she replies saying that she has no husband. The response, then, of the Lord that touched the woman's heart and changed her life was,

> *"You are right in saying, 'I have no husband;' for you have had five husbands, and he whom you now have is not your husband...."* (verses 17&18).

This resulted in the power of God coming upon her with such conviction that she dropped her water jug and ran back to the village. Then with great excitement she shared the good news of Jesus saying,

> *"Come, see a man, who told me all that I ever did. Can this be the Christ?"* (verse 29).

Further on in the account we read the outcome of this message was,

> *"Many Samaritans from that city believed in Him because of the woman's testimony...."* (verse 39).

The most unlikely person was used by God and, in the same way, the Lord is able to use us, regardless of our background or our reputation. He takes individuals who feel they have little to offer, those who consider that they couldn't make much of a difference, and through their lives He does amazing things. Just like the small lad with his few loaves and fishes that fed 5,000 people. When the little we have is placed into the hands of the Lord, the most unexpected things can happen, as God meets the needs of others through us.

One of the wonderful things about a personal testimony is that nobody can argue against what God has evidently done in our lives. This is true whether it is the intellectual who wants to make us appear foolish with his clever arguments, the great philosopher who may try to overwhelm us with his deep and lofty ideas, or even the hardened sceptic who stubbornly resists all reason. None of these can stand against our personal testimony, where we can say, *"I know it's true, because it happened to me!"*

(C) *The Power of God To Destroy The Works of The Devil*
Demons are just as real today as they were in the days of the Bible; they haven't died out. Satanic activity, creating strongholds in people's lives, even in the lives of Christians, is very real. The enemy sows his lies, paralyses people with fear, undermines their confidence, brings oppression, and afflicts them with sickness. Paul believed in the reality of Satan's activity against Christians, which is why he said to the Ephesian Church,

> *"For we are not contending against flesh and blood, but against the principalities, against the powers, against the world rulers of this present darkness, against the spiritual hosts of wickedness in the heavenly places."*

(Ephesians 6:12).

Peter also realised what the enemy was able to do, even against believers, and so he wrote a warning to them saying,

> *"Be self-controlled and alert. Your enemy the devil prowls around like a roaring lion looking for someone to devour."*

(1 Peter 5:8, NIV).

When we are walking, submitted to the claims of the gospel, surrendered completely to Christ as Lord, then the enemy can have no victory over us whatsoever. But, if there is disobedience, wrong attitudes and any form of sin in our lives, this places us in an extremely dangerous position where we are wide open to the enemy's attack.

This is why the glorious gospel message is so important and relevant to our daily needs. The good news reminds us that,

"For this purpose the Son of God was manifested, that He might destroy the works of the devil." (1 John 3:8b, AV).

When we feel oppressed and under attack from the enemy we can come to Jesus as Lord, acknowledge the provision and power of the gospel to set us free, then the yoke that the enemy has put upon us can be broken.

In the book of Revelation, John spoke about the victory believers would have over the devil and all his evil forces. He made clear the importance of a present application and experience of the gospel in the believer's life by saying,

"And they have conquered him, by the blood of the Lamb and by the word of their testimony, for they loved not their lives even unto death." (Revelation 12:11).

Thirdly, A PERSONAL APPROPRIATION

We need to bring into our experience that which God has so clearly promised in His word, and so richly provided through the cross. This is why, *"the gospel is the power of God for salvation, to **every one who has faith**".*

GOD HAS NO FAVOURITES

The Bible gives us tremendous assurance that what has been promised in the scriptures is for our lives today. It says,

"For all the promises of God find their yes in Him."
(2 Corinthians 1:20).

Every single promise is available for us to experience, we just need to appropriate it. The cross of Christ is our guarantee that what has been paid for at such a high price will most definitely be granted to us. Paul speaks of this in saying,

*"He that spared not His own Son, but delivered Him up
for us all, how shall He not with Him also freely give us all
things?"* (Romans 8:32, AV).

Our trust must be in the message of the cross which is at the very
heart of the gospel. The cross is not something we merely sing sweetly
about, or that we decoratively wear, nor is it something we just
religiously look to. The cross is the power of God! This is why Paul
said,

*"For the preaching of the cross is foolishness to those who
are perishing, but **to those who believe,** it is the power of
God."* (1 Corinthians 1:18).

Whilst it is a fact that God has no favourites, He does, however,
respond to faith. Those who are more likely to experience His power
are the ones who believe. These are the people who, when they are sick,
come with determination to the cross to appropriate their healing. When
they are crushed by defeat, they come humbly, that they may rise up in
victory. When there is fear in their lives, they come confidently to be
released. When they are convicted of sin, they come repentant to the
cross to be forgiven and set free.

The people who believe, demonstrate their faith by coming to
receive God's provision. They don't come to the cross in a sentimental,
superficial, or a self-pitying way, they come simply, but with certainty,
to receive God's power personally into their lives.

The great British evangelist Gypsy Smith was once asked the
question, *"How do you start a revival?"* He thought for a moment and
then answered in these terms, he said,

*"Go home, lock yourself in your room, kneel down in the
middle of your floor and draw a chalk mark around yourself.
Then ask God to begin the revival, inside the chalk mark.
When the Lord has answered your prayer, the revival will be
on!"*

We must personally bring into our own lives God's provision for
ourselves, and appropriate all that is promised by faith. The gospel is

the power of God to <u>every one</u> who has "FAITH". We shall be looking more closely at the subject of faith in the next chapter, but this is the key that unlocks the blessing of God. Bible faith demands that we do something.

As far as God is concerned action speaks louder than words, which is why James says,
"So faith by itself, if it has no works, is dead."
(James 2:17).

It is not enough just to declare that we believe by raising our hands, or our voices as we pray. The 'bottom line' is, our faith will be seen in what we do.

D. L. Moody gives us a fine example of someone's faith being expressed in actions. Before he became a famous evangelist, he started a Sunday school in a public hall above a city market.

During the week he worked as a travelling salesman, selling boots and shoes. But he always returned to Chicago by Saturday night. The next morning he would rise at 6.00 a.m. to get the hall ready for Sunday school. He would move out the beer kegs and arrange the chairs. Then he'd go out on the streets to find children for the class. By 2.00 p.m. he would have the hall filled. After dismissing the group, he would go and visit all the absentees, talk to their parents about the Lord, and call on people who were sick.

If we have real faith it will be expressed in how we think, feel, speak and act, especially in difficult circumstances. This is something I was reminded of during a ministry trip to East Africa. I recall being surprised there by someone, who was always known as a 'man of faith,' and yet he didn't quite live up to his reputation. Throughout our stay in Tanzania this person was constantly anxious about the food he was eating, the water he was drinking and the sanitary conditions. Frequently he would be expressing his worries through negative remarks.

Walking in the power of the gospel, however, alters our whole perspective, because we know that it changes lives, impacts cities, destroys the works of Satan, and equips us for more effective service. We will personally know a greater measure of that power when **firstly,** there is a Positive Identification, compelling us to say, *"I am not ashamed of the gospel."* **Secondly,** we have a Present Realisation, enabling us to declare with conviction, *"for it is the power of God for salvation."* And **thirdly,** we make a Personal Appropriation, as we are convinced, God's power is *"to every one who has faith".*

Chapter 9

Fuelling The Flame Of Faith

The farcical story is told of a woman who regularly attended a church that had a strong emphasis on faith in their teaching. One Sunday morning she arrived without her husband and was asked by the pastor, *"Where is Tom today?"*

"Oh, he's home sick," came the reply from the woman.

"No, no!" said the pastor sternly, *"He's not sick; he just thinks he's sick!"*

The woman, feeling somewhat guilty at her apparent lapse of faith, responded apologetically, saying, *"Oh, I'm sorry, I'll have to tell him that when I get home."*

The following week, when she came back to the church, she was again by herself, and as the pastor greeted her at the door, he asked once more, *"Is Tom not with you today?"*

"No, I'm afraid he's not; replied the woman, *he thinks he's dead!"*

Although this sounds somewhat ridiculous, this is actually the foolish extreme that some 'faith teachers' are in danger of misleading people into. Maintaining a positive confession is all very well and needs to be encouraged, but in the extreme it can develop into a form of self-deception that denies the reality of indisputable evidence. Such deception inevitably leads at least to disappointment, and also possible harm.

If we are to realise our full potential we will do so, not by living in a realm of denial or pretence, but by facing up to every dark challenge life brings and overcoming it with the bright flame of genuine faith.

The wise counsel given to the disciples by Jesus was, *"Have faith in God."* (Mark 11:22b). He wanted them to develop into all they had the potential of being, and to achieve everything He had purposed for them. To do this though, they had to be sure that their faith was not in methods, techniques, or even faith in faith itself. Their dependence had to be wholly on God.

The Lord wants each one of us to have a faith that burns brightly and not one that flickers faintly. This is a faith that is able to destroy the darkness of Satan's lies, dispel the shadows of doubt and discouragement, and draw others to the light of our testimony concerning Christ. For faith to be genuine, (that is coming from the right source) and if it is to burn brightly, then we must take care that we are fuelling it with spiritual principles.

Firstly, LISTENING TO THE RIGHT THINGS
When talking about the fuel of faith, the Bible tells us,
> *"Faith comes from what is heard, and what is heard comes by the preaching of Christ."* (Romans 10:17).

There are so many harmful things around our lives today that try to extinguish the flame of faith. Among them are: the evil attack of ungodly words, nagging doubts, deceptive whispers, and negative comments. These all contradict God's word and can influence what we believe.

(A) *Ungodly Words*
For a long period of time, (almost always whilst I was away ministering), my wife used to receive anonymous phone calls. These were abusive and ungodly calls that the enemy was trying to use to bring oppression and darkness into our home.

During this time I also received an abusive letter, from a so-called Christian, that again had this aim of casting a shadow over our lives. Enclosed in the envelope was one of my handbills showing a publicity photograph, and the sender had coloured in the picture of myself with a black marker. He had drawn horns coming out of my head, a trident in

150

my hand and had given me a forked tail. In the letter he said that I was *"a demon-possessed I.R.A. terrorist"* and, *"a bastard of Satan"*.

You can imagine the darkness that was trying to come against our ministry through words filled with such hatred.

God's word, however, brings tremendous encouragement, even in some of the blackest moments of our lives. This is so, whether it's at times of personal attack, physical sickness or problems that leave us feeling full of despair. When we fuel the flame of faith with what God says, then we are fully persuaded that no matter how deep the darkness might seem, He is always greater than that darkness.

(B) *Nagging Doubts*

Only a few days ago whilst speaking at a meeting in Staffordshire, a man came forward for prayer. He was in leadership and had a preaching ministry, but nagging doubts were tormenting him concerning a major step of faith he had taken. He shared that deep depression would seize him, making him feel suicidal, and each morning he would wake up and actually pray that he might die. That night, as he listened to God's word, he was reminded of the truth of the gospel that he could be set free. We prayed together for the yoke of oppression to be broken by the Lord and he was released from his dark prison of doubt.

This was the case also for a woman sitting in the congregation at a meeting in Manchester. She looked extremely dark and oppressed with her problems and, after the service, came out for prayer. She shared that her husband, who was a Methodist minister, had left her and their family to set up home with another woman.

She had come into the meeting feeling depressed and tormented by a sense of failure regarding the past, and troubled by nagging doubts for the future. Before going home though, she said, *"Thank you so much, I needed to hear God's word this morning. At first I felt full of despair, but as I've been listening it's brought hope back into my heart."*

(C) *Deceptive Whispers*

Listening to the wrong things not only weakens our faith, it also leaves us wide open to deception, and takes us away from God. A lady who came for prayer from the Midlands was in this position. She had been a Christian for many years but confessed that her life was a mess. Although married with young children, she had been having an affair with a Christian man, from another church, for several years. At first she knew that what they were doing was wrong, but the deceptive whispers of Satan had caused her to rationalise her actions to the point where it no longer seemed so serious.

This continued until she became pregnant as a result of her adultery, and only three days before speaking to me she had an abortion. It was then that the full consequences of her sin started to hit her. The woman was full of guilt and shame for what she had done, and the flame of faith in her life had all but gone out. That morning, though, she was not only convicted, but as she listened to God's word, she also found God's mercy. By responding in repentance she was able to receive the forgiveness and restoration of the one who, *".... a dimly burning wick He will not quench"*. (Isaiah 42:3).

(D) *Negative Comments*

If our heart is not set on God and being fuelled by faith, it will be extremely vulnerable to the power of fear and will readily absorb negative words. Fearful people are, more often than not, those who feed on pessimistic things. When we allow any negativity into our lives it will always weaken our faith and make us reluctant to move into God's full provision. This is what happened to Israel when they listened to the report from the spies who went in to view the promised land. On hearing their assessment that they would be defeated because the people were stronger, giants were in the land, and the cities were fortified, their confidence melted away dramatically:

> *"Then all the congregation raised a loud cry; and the people wept that night. And all the people of Israel murmured against Moses and Aaron....'Would that we had died in the land of Egypt! Or would that we had died in this*

wilderness! ..... Our wives and our little ones will become a prey; would it not be better for us to go back to Egypt?'"
(Numbers 14:1-3).

When we are committed to refuse negativity any entrance into our lives, we will begin to think and feel radically different. Listening instead to the positive faith of others, who have proved God themselves, and hearing also what His word says we are able to accomplish, inspires us to press on.

Secondly, BELIEVING THE RIGHT THINGS

In the 1920's an old Pentecostal chorus was written that fired up the faith of Christians then, and has done so ever since. The words, based on Scripture, are, *"Only believe, only believe, all things are possible only believe"*. Often people wonder whether life can really be as simple as that. Well, the short answer is yes, but it depends entirely on what you are believing. There are Christians today who believe the wrong things. They build their lives upon the shaky foundation of their feelings, circumstances, logic, the opinions of others, and the lies of the enemy; instead of believing God's word.

True faith must be built on the solid foundation of God's character, a fundamental aspect of which is His integrity; He does not lie. This is established in Numbers 23:19; in fact, the whole of our Christian experience thus far, and all we long to be in the future, rests upon this one verse. By believing it we fuel the flame of faith:
> *"God is not a man, that He should lie, nor a son of man, that He should change His mind. Does He speak and then not act? Does He promise and not fulfil?"* (NIV).

The Truth Will Always Ultimately Triumph

Not only is everything God says absolutely true, it will also certainly come to pass for us as we walk in the truth of His word. The truth of what God says will always triumph, even over trouble. Nowhere is this victory more clearly demonstrated than in Christ, who is the truth, at Calvary's cross. There at the cross all the darkness and torment of trouble conspired against the Son of God. One of the titles given to the Lord that speaks of this trouble is,

"…. *man of sorrows, and acquainted with grief.*"

(Isaiah 53:3).

When we look at Jesus we see someone who was rejected by the very people He came to help. He was betrayed by someone He trusted, denied by another who claimed complete allegiance, abused and humiliated by those He wanted to restore dignity to. Then, having been put to an agonising death, Jesus was laid in a sealed tomb. This was man's final statement that they had destroyed the truth of God. Praise the Lord though, for the resurrection! It is in this historic event that we see the greatest example of the truth triumphing over trouble.

For each believer, rising up victorious and reigning with Christ over every difficult situation is made possible for us because of the nature of truth, which is undefeatable. Truth is not merely a body of doctrine, or some theoretical principle; it is a miracle-working, life-changing, need-meeting power! This is why Jesus said,

"You will know the truth, and the truth will make you free."

(John 8:32).

The truth of God's word has a liberating power to set us free from all that is contrary to His will for our lives. This liberating power though, is only ever activated when we *"know"* the truth; that is a heart experience brought alive by the Holy Spirit.

The Truth Is Greater Than The Facts

Living in the power of God's truth should cause people to have great confidence, conviction and clarity regarding the Lord's will for their lives. The reason why sometimes this is not the case though, is because some Christians are confused and mistaken in what they believe. People too easily accept facts to be the truth. This is a great mistake, because facts are not always the truth. Facts are natural, and the truth is supernatural.

154

The trouble of our difficult circumstances and how we may feel at the moment might well be a fact, but it is not greater than the truth of God's word. For example, the trouble of difficult relationships, ill health, financial struggles, insecurity, depression, loneliness, failure etc. may well be undeniable, but the truth of what God can do is more powerful. We have to choose which to put our faith in, the facts, or the truth. The truth is able to change the facts but, praise God, facts can never change the truth!

While we continue to believe the facts about our marriage, family, health, ministry and future prospects etc., rather than the truth of what God says, we will never develop into all that He has planned for us to be.

The Bible is full of people who refused to believe only what they could see in terms of the evidence around them. Instead, they chose to believe the truth of God's word and their testimony still stands as a bright beacon of hope to encourage us today.

Abraham is one such person. The facts surrounding his life were undeniable; they were obvious to all. He was a hundred years of age and, as far as his prospects of fathering children were concerned, the Bible plainly says,
    ".... his body was as good as dead."   (Romans 4:19a).

The added particulars of his circumstances were that his wife Sarah was 90 years old, and barren in her womb. Yet in spite of this glaring evidence, the truth of God's word had promised that Abraham's seed was going to be numbered as the stars of heaven and the sand of the seashore. (Genesis 22:17). God had said that from this man would come nations, and even kings. (Genesis17:6).

Because Abraham chose to believe the truth of God's word rather than the facts of his circumstances, God was able to bring to pass what He had promised.

The Lord is still the same today; He looks for those who will believe His word over and above whatever the facts may say. This is not, as we warned against at the beginning of the chapter, *denying* the existence of indisputable evidence. It is *deciding* to believe that whatever God says has ultimate power over every fact, and because of this they are subject to change. It is through those who live by faith and not by sight, that miracles will be birthed, prophecies shall come to pass and promises will be fulfilled.

Thirdly, SEEING THE RIGHT THINGS

(A) *Seeing Ourselves As We Truly Are*

Sometimes the perception we have of ourselves is very different from how others see us. This point was made clear to me over a year ago when visiting the opticians for my first eye test since leaving school. As the receptionist was filling in my details, she asked what my age was, and without thinking I replied, *"Thirty-three, thirty-four in September."* She made no response to this and simply completed the necessary information.

Whilst being examined by the optician though, he looked into my eyes, then back at the form, and with a puzzled expression asked, *"How old did you say you were?"*

Again, I answered, *"Thirty-three."*

Then in a tone of disbelief he said to me, *"There's something not quite right here; you have the eyes of at least a forty year old"*.

It was at that moment I realised my mistake; I wasn't thirty-three, I was forty-three!

In a similar way, we all need at times to have a spiritual eye check, to determine how clearly we are seeing things. It is under the close examination of the expert that our true condition is brought to light. Responding to what the Lord reveals about ourselves, is the only way we can move forward towards our destiny, and this requires honesty.

A Christian leader who came out for prayer at a meeting in Lancashire, realised the importance of this. In front of all his congregation he admitted there was no joy in his life. He shared that he had lost his motivation and was responding for prayer because he needed help.

It would have been so easy for him to have carried on going through the motions and hiding the truth from his church, but he longed for reality. Not only did God powerfully touch him that night, his honesty brought a response from the rest of the congregation to seek help as well.

One of the major hindrances to a person realising their full potential is how they view themselves. If someone has a low opinion of their worth and their ability then this will restrict them greatly. It is virtually impossible for faith to function effectively in the heart of a person with a poor self-image. Such people are constantly feeling inadequate to overcome life's challenges, and ill-equipped to grasp life's opportunities.

This was the case for Israel when the opportunity of the promised land lay before them. The prospect of overcoming the army that stood in-between them and God's provision seemed too daunting a prospect. They defeated themselves before even a blow had been struck because of their 'grasshopper mentality'. The Bible records the perception they had of themselves when they said,
"....we were in our own sight as grasshoppers, and so we were in their sight." (Numbers 13:33, AV).

When we do not see ourselves as God does we are believing a lie. This restricts us internally, and also communicates externally to everyone, including the enemy, that we are prepared to settle for less than God's best. It was because Israel saw themselves in an insignificant, weak way that the enemy also viewed them accordingly. We should be able to walk tall, with great security, because of the value God places upon us. He sees us as unique individuals, of tremendous worth, and so ought we. To each of His children God says,
".... you are precious in my eyes and honoured, and I love you." (Isaiah 43:4a).

This confidence in his worth as a unique individual was something that the psalmist, David, had. When thinking of the incredible nature of God's creation he asks the question,

> *"What is man that thou art mindful of him, and the son of man that thou dost care for him?"* (Psalm 8:4).

Then having pondered this, he comes to a conclusion and says,

> *"Yet thou hast made him little less than God, and dost crown him with glory and honour. Thou hast given him dominion over the works of thy hands; thou hast put all things under his feet...."* (verses 5&6).

(B) *Seeing God As He Truly Is*

When we see God as He truly is, it fuels the flame of faith, giving us greater confidence to come to Him with our needs. This is what He was encouraging His people to do when He spoke to them through the prophet Jeremiah. Even though Israel had sinned greatly against God, still He said to them,

> *"Call me, and I will answer thee, and show thee great and mighty things, which thou knowest not."*

> (Jeremiah 33:3, AV).

This verse shows us that there are certain things we need to see about God that help to strengthen our faith.

God Often Waits For The Cry Of Our Heart

In verse 3, we have a wonderful invitation to reach out beyond ourselves to the Lord. God says, *"Call me....."* You would think, surely no-one would ever need reminding of this, and yet we do. Sometimes we try to struggle on, neglecting our relationship with Him, acting as though we were the answer to our own problems, and putting our trust in other people or other things for security, rather than God.

The Lord knows our situation; He has not forgotten us, but sometimes our needs go unmet, the solution is unfound, our desires are unfulfilled and our prayers are unanswered, because God is waiting. It is as if He is stepping back until we completely turn to Him, really meaning what we say as we call out in prayer.

158

When Peter started to walk on water he began to get into difficulty and so he shouted desperately for help. The scripture says, *".... beginning to sink he cried out ....."* (Matthew 14:30).

The shortest most heartfelt prayer in the Bible was heard at this moment when he said, *"Lord, save me!"* Peter's desperation was prompted by the realisation of his urgent need. Sometimes we never really seek God with all our hearts, trust in Him alone and truly cry out in prayer, until we realise we are beginning to sink! It is when we see that without God's intervention we are going under, that we get desperate and call out for help.

What tends to dull our sense of urgency, and expression of desperation, is quite simply that we are often too comfortable, without any real need of God. It is at times like this that the Lord allows a crisis to come into our lives so that we become aware once more of how much we really need Him.

The one thing you will never see in the life of a drowning man is apathy and indifference. Someone that is going under for the third or fourth time, gasping their last breath, quickly becomes serious and wholehearted in their call for help.

When we are beginning to sink, our perspective and priorities dramatically change. This was tragically illustrated in the account of what happened with the sinking of the Titanic. Up until the moment of crisis little thought was given to God, but when the boat was going down, the song that the band struck up wasn't the latest jazz number, or pop song; it was the old hymn, *"Nearer my God to thee."*

It is in the time of crisis that the things we spent our life pursuing and holding onto so tightly become meaningless, and that which we paid little attention or regard to, becomes the most precious and important.

God Is Willing To Meet Our Need

Verse 3 says, *".... I will answer you."* What is important for us to be assured of, particularly when trouble challenges our faith, is the willingness of God, not only to hear our cry, but also to answer. Often people are unsure about the will of God and it is because of this that they find it difficult to pray with any conviction. This uncertainty must be dispelled because it will always dampen the flame of faith.

The will of God is found in the word of God; as we look into the scriptures what we are reading is God's last will and testament. It is as we take Him at His word that our faith is increased and our needs are met. The way God answers might not always be what we want, but it will always be what is best for us, and what we need.

Our faith stands on the sure foundation that God is more willing to give than, very often, we are to receive. In fact, He throws out a personal challenge to prove Him in Malachi chapter 3. Here God states that if we take care not to rob Him of all that is His due, then He will gladly shower us with His blessing:

> "..... put me to the test, says the Lord of hosts, if I will not
> open the windows of heaven for you and pour down for you
> an overflowing blessing."   (verse 10b).

Furthermore, the willingness of God to respond to our cry is made clear in our understanding of Him as our Heavenly Father. It is because people can sometimes only relate to God in His majesty, glory and power that they fail to see a God who is willing to respond to them, not just at a time of crisis, but wanting to give good things to them regardless.

I can remember preaching at a church in Kent where one of the leaders had this problem. That evening I was speaking on the fatherhood of God and he came to me afterwards saying, *"I cannot relate to God as father, as you spoke of tonight, because we had a father in our family who ruled with a rod of iron; he ruled by fear!"*

If a person has had the experience of having an earthly father who is cold, unresponsive and hard, then it dramatically affects the way they see God as their father.

People today seem to have a very distorted image of God. While preparing for a crusade near Deal in Kent, I was being interviewed on the radio and it gave a tremendous opportunity to share the gospel with many people. The questions being put to me made it simple to speak about Christ, at least that was until the interviewer asked something very strange. He said, *"Do you think it is fair on the people of that area to bring the gospel of Christ to them?"*

What an extraordinary question! For a few seconds it left me without an answer, because it was so unexpected and unusual. This shows the distorted image that people often have in their minds about God. They see Him as someone who wants to spoil people's enjoyment, restrict their freedom, and impose upon them something that is undesirable. This, of course, could not be further from the truth.

When Jesus was speaking about the willingness of God to respond to people's needs, it was the image of a loving father, deeply committed to the welfare of His children, that He referred to. He said:

"What man of you, if his son asks him for bread, will give
him a stone? Or if he asks for a fish, will give him a serpent?
If you then, who are evil, know how to give good gifts to your
children, how much more will your Father who is in heaven
give good gifts to those who ask Him!"

(Matthew 7:9-11).

Jesus gave two other reasons why we should be assured of the willingness of God to meet our needs. When we come on the basis of these promises and understand these reasons then we can know great confidence. The first promise Jesus spoke of relates to God being glorified by His response to our prayer. He said,

"Whatever you ask in my name, I will do it, that the
Father may be glorified in the Son." (John 14:13).

The other reason relates to our own experience of joy. It takes into consideration the importance of us being filled with the knowledge of a God who cares and wants to be involved in our life. Jesus said,

"Hitherto you have asked nothing in my name; ask, and
you will receive, that your joy may be full." (John 16:24).

God Wants To Bring Greater Revelation Into Our Lives

Having invited us to call to Him, and assured us of His willingness to respond, God then goes on to say in verse 3 that there was something else He wanted to do:

".....and show thee great and mighty things, which thou knowest not."

There is a great deal that we do not know, and much that we have yet to move into. If our faith is to be strengthened we need to be sure that God wants to reveal to us His purpose for our lives. Revelation is a vital fuel to our faith. Our lives can change more in just a moment of revelation, than a life-time of studying the Bible. Important though studying is, on its own it is insufficient, compared to the understanding we receive as the Lord, by His Holy Spirit, reveals truth to us. It is revelation that keeps us spiritually fresh and with a sharp, cutting edge to our testimony.

We see the importance of revelation when Jesus said to His disciples, *"..... Who do men say that the Son of Man is?"* (Matthew 16:13b). Even though this was the initial question that Jesus asked, He was not interested in mere speculation, or information. Having heard that some were saying He was John the Baptist, and others Elijah, Jeremiah, or one of the prophets, Jesus then goes on to ask, *".... But who do you say that I am?"* (verse 15).

Peter was the first to reply with a personal confession of faith in Jesus as the Christ, to which the Lord says,

".... For flesh and blood has not revealed this to you, but my Father who is in heaven." (verse 17b).

We notice from this that what strengthens people's faith is not speculation or information, but revelation, and it is out of our relationship with the Lord that revelation comes. The closer we are walking with Him the more clearly we understand His will. Jesus delights to make known all that we need to help our lives grow strong. To those who were in relationship with Him He said, *"..... all that I have heard from my Father, I have made known to you."* (John 15:15b).

Meeting our needs is important to God, but ultimately He desires us not just to *want His provision,* but also to *walk in His purpose.* We saw in an earlier chapter that one of the greatest leaders ever to be born was looking after sheep on a hillside when God called him. Even though he was one of the most unlikely candidates to be used in any significant way, God was about to change all that. The Lord wanted to reveal something about his future so that this man would discover his destiny.

In looking at the facts that stood against this prospect we see they really were quite enormous: Moses had no confidence, no experience, no credibility, no past success record, and on top of this, he had a speech impediment. In his own estimation, and certainly in the eyes of others, he was far from being suitable leadership material.

However, nothing can stop us being what God wants us to be once we, by revelation, see the greatness of the plan He has for us. We need to have faith that God has got a very special purpose for our lives, and if we will co-operate with Him, He will take the responsibility for working that out. He tells us in His word,
> *"For I know the plans I have for you, says the Lord, plans for welfare and not for evil, to give you a future and a hope."*
> (Jeremiah 29:11).

Fourthly, **EXPRESSING THE RIGHT THINGS**
Sometimes the things we express come out of frustration, hurt and discouragement rather than faith. This reminds me of an amusing story about a man who had no joy in his life. He was so fed up one Sunday morning that he refused to get out of bed. His mother tried in vain to stir him, saying that he was going to be late for church, but still he wouldn't get up.

Finally, she shouted up the stairs, *"Just give me two reasons why you don't want to go?"*

The son then replied, *"I'm not getting up, and I don't want to go to church because I don't like the people, and the people don't like me! You give me two reasons why I should go."*

"Well, that's easy," said the mother, *"first of all you're 50 years of age, and secondly, you are the vicar!!"*

Faith and joy are inseparable, and one without the other is incomplete. When faith is in our heart, then regardless of what is going on around us, or coming against us, that faith will be expressed in what we say. The apostle Paul knew the importance and power of expressing the right things which is why he stated,

"Since we have the same spirit of faith as he had who wrote, 'I believed, therefore I spoke,' we too believe, and so we speak." (2 Corinthians 4:13).

We have previously said, in earlier chapters, that joy comes from knowing the presence of God, and liberty in the Holy Spirit releases joy in our lives. What we are looking at now is that the flame of faith is kept burning brightly by committing ourselves to praise the Lord at all times.

The devil wants to keep us quiet and shut us up, but our faith is strengthened as we declare the praises of God, even in difficult circumstances. Billy Bray was a living example of someone who refused to remain silent. He was a Cornish tin miner in the 19th Century who became a preacher. He used to say, *"I'd rather be among the shouters than the doubters!"*

People often would get offended at his enthusiasm and they would persecute him for his faith, even physically attack him. In the light of such a prospect he would remark, *"Even if people grab hold of me, put me in a barrel and roll me down a hill, I'll still shout 'glory!' out of the bung hole!"*

Another of his sayings was, *"I can't help praising the Lord! As I go along the street, I lift up one foot and it seems to say, 'Glory!' and I lift up the other and it seems to say, 'Amen!' And so they keep on like that all the time I'm walking!"*

The expression of our faith should not only be audible, it should be visible too; it ought to be evident on our face. A challenging Christian song was written a few years ago that had the rather pointed words, *"If you're happy please inform your face."* When the joy of Jesus is a reality in our lives then it will be evident for all to see. That's why the Bible says, *"A glad heart makes a cheerful countenance."* (Proverbs 15:13a).

Imagine what would happen if in every church a huge mirror, right behind the preacher, was installed. People would then see the measure of their own enthusiasm and interest, and I'm sure in some cases they would be quite shocked!

The expression of joyful praise is not just about volume; it is an attitude of heart. This is how the prophet Habakkuk lived. All around his life there were depressing circumstances. Everything looked negative, his prayers didn't seem to be answered and he was going through a barren time. In spite of such deep darkness though, the bright expression of his faith is seen in his attitude to praise the Lord, even when it was hard to do so. He said:

> *"Though the fig tree do not blossom, nor fruit be on the vines, the produce of the olive fail and the fields yield no food, the flock be cut off from the fold and there be no herd in the stalls, yet I will rejoice in the Lord, I will joy in the God of my salvation."* (Habakkuk 3:17&18).

There is power in praise! This is because joy is not merely an emotion, it is a spiritual force that accomplishes at least three things in our lives:

(A) *It Brings A Spiritual Strength To The Individual*
Christians who have little evidence of joy in their lives will always be weak and easily defeated. Joy is essential in strengthening us to stand against trials and to resist temptation. This is revealed when the Bible says, *".... the joy of the Lord is your strength."* (Nehemiah 8:10b).

The energising power of joy doesn't come through something we work up ourselves, or because of the rhythm and beat of a good rousing song; it is *"the joy of the Lord"*. It can only be experienced when we

165

remain in the centre of God's will and we walk in obedience to His word.

This same joy is spoken of in Hebrews 12: 2. Referring to Jesus the writer says,

> *"…. who for the joy that was set before Him endured the cross, despising the shame, and is seated at the right hand of the throne of God."*

That kind of joy will get us through the darkest of circumstances, right through to the place of victory, just as it did for the Lord. It will be a major factor in helping us fulfil our destiny and is not dependent on our emotions; it is supernaturally imparted by God.

(B) *It Stimulates Faith In Others*

When we maintain a joyful consistency, even when life is difficult, then other people begin to take notice of our faith. They will be impressed and attracted by the genuineness of what they see. In a world living without God, where there isn't much to be joyful about, joy draws them to want to know for themselves this reality.

The Psalmist, when speaking about his faith, testified to what God had done for him, saying,

> *"He put a new song in my mouth, a song of praise to our God. **Many** will see and fear, and put their trust in the Lord."*   (Psalm 40:3).

The power of this joy is such that it doesn't only affect a few, God's word speaks about *"Many"* being influenced and brought to faith in the Lord.

(C) *It Shatters The Power Of The Enemy*

We have already seen that the message of the gospel destroys the works of the devil. Also one other very effective weapon is the power of joy in our lives; this breaks his hold on us as well. There is nothing greater than praise to unlock prison doors and overcome all our enemies. The devil triumphs over the child of God who has little joy because he has weakened his faith through things like discouragement,

166

disappointment and despair. However, the believer who knows how to rejoice in adversity has a supernatural power that always brings defeat to the works of darkness.

In 2 Chronicles 20:21&22 we read about the Israelites going into a battle against an army much bigger than themselves, and were it not for God being with them, they would have been easily defeated. God gave them a strategy though for winning the battle, and as they followed it carefully, victory was assured. They were instructed to put the singers and dancers right at the front of the army, as the spearhead for their advance. It was as they went forward singing and dancing that the enemy was conquered and victory was established.

We also will know great victories, and live outstanding lives, when we stand out in what we believe. God wants the flame of faith in us to burn brightly and not flicker faintly. This flame is fuelled when we believe that the truth of His word will always triumph. In trouble and difficult circumstances God often waits for the cry of our heart. He is willing to meet our need, and He wants to bring greater revelation into our lives. It is in knowing these truths that we are set free to a new place of faith, joy and confidence to be all that He has planned for us to be.

Chapter 10

Peace In The Midst Of Problems

Recently I heard the true story of a father who decided to go out for dinner with his three young daughters. Battling against the bustle of people in the busy restaurant he took the hand of his excited children, and led them through the food line. Juggling with everyone's plates and drinks, he instructed each one to be on their best behaviour. When they were all finally seated, he sighed with relief and told them they were doing great, that they hadn't had any *'catastrophes'* yet. At the mention of this, his three year old daughter, eager to help, looked around and volunteered saying, *"Where are they, Daddy? I'll go get them!"*

When I heard this I had to smile at the amusing innocence of the remark. For us though, with perhaps more enlightened eyes, we know life is not so carefree.

There are not many things certain today, but one thing we can be sure of is that we will all experience problems, even *'catastrophes,'* and we will not have to go in search of them either; they will find us! Jesus pointed this out to His disciples when He said, *"In this world you will have trouble ....."* (John 16:33b).

The very thing that is common to every person is what prevents so many from realising their full potential, and fulfilling their destiny. It is because of this that God gives the wonderful gift of His peace to uphold and sustain those who look to Him.

Albert Einstein, the German-born, American physicist once said, *"Peace cannot be kept by force, it can only be achieved by understanding"*. This is indeed so, but only when that understanding is established on the foundation of spiritual insight, rather than human reason.

Some people, even in the Church, have a strange understanding that peace and problems are mutually exclusive of one another. They tend to believe that there will be times when they have peace and times when they will have problems, and these two experiences are considered quite separate. The miracle of God's grace though, is that we can know peace in the midst of problems. Regardless of what comes against us, and in spite of the trials we go through, we can know God's peace in every situation.

A lot is said by many today about peace, yet we see such little evidence of it. Peace summits are held, agreements reached, and treaties are signed, but still peace seems to elude mankind. It would appear to be extremely fragile and all too fleeting. While we thank God for those who work for the cause of peace, not just in the Middle East or Northern Ireland, but throughout the world, the Bible warns us about having a false sense of security. It says,
> *"While people are saying, 'Peace and safety,' destruction*
> *will come on them suddenly...."* (1 Thessalonians 5:3, NIV).

True peace cannot be found if we are looking for the wrong thing, in the wrong place, through the wrong means. It was Herbert Hoover, America's 31st President, who said, while holding office during the Great Depression: *"Peace is not made at the council tables, or by treaties, but in the hearts of men."*

Peace is not the absence of noise, nor what happens when two warring armies come to a cease-fire. It is an inner quality of life that is independent of our circumstances, but totally dependent upon Jesus being Lord of all. Therefore, any part of our lives where Jesus is not Lord will be an area in which we will not know true peace.

One key verse to consider in relation to this is Colossians 3:15. Here Paul says,
> *"Let the peace of Christ rule in your hearts, to which*
> *indeed you were called...."*

From this we learn that we have not been destined to be driven by our mood swings, nor doomed to be dominated by our circumstances. What will keep us in God's will, living consistently in victory, is when our hearts are ruled by His peace.

In an age of uncertainty, insecurity and change, the pressure of problems is all around us in daily life. There is great pressure on marriage and the family, pressure on young people in schools, pressure at work, and pressure in the ministry. Even with all our sophistication, advance in technology, and material security, the three most predominant characteristics of our time are worry, fear and stress. These are related to each other, and progressive in nature; one leads to the other and then on to the next. They go from bad to worse.

WORRY - This, according to 'Webster's Dictionary of Words,' means, *"To torment oneself with disturbing thoughts, to feel uneasy, anxious and troubled"*. We all know that worry never does us any good, in fact, it only magnifies the problem that we dwell on, blowing out of all proportion the concerns we have. It eats away at us as we turn over and over in our minds every detail and facet of what troubles us. Even though this is so, still it is something that we all seem to do.

J. Arthur Rank, who succeeded so well in the film industry, devised a practical way of handling the problem of worry. Not having enough faith to overcome his troubles immediately, he decided that the next best thing was to postpone thinking about them until his mind had cleared. So when something disturbing occurred, he wrote the problem on a card and would not dwell on it until a little time had passed. Then when he reviewed all the difficulties that had been of such great concern a week or so before, he found to his surprise that most of them had already disappeared.

He therefore concluded that much of his distress was a waste of energy and a loss of sleep, for God had intervened and directed his life.

FEAR - This is a very strong and powerful emotion; it is like faith in reverse gear. Fear will always send our thoughts racing in a direction that is in conflict with faith. Where faith wants us to arrive at, and be secure in, fear will take our lives the opposite way. It is a preoccupation with what might adversely affect ourselves, or those that we love; a dwelling upon what *'could'* go wrong, what *'might'* happen, and how things *'perhaps, may'* develop. With our imagination we project our thoughts into the future so that we fear the worst. When we are doing this, the fear of the unknown becomes a major bondage and our potential is paralysed.

STRESS - This is usually caused by an inner conflict of emotions, or an outward clash of personality, and it is almost always our negative reaction to the build-up of circumstances and events. No amount of difficult circumstances can bring stress into our life; it is how we handle them that determines this. A negative reaction will always open wide the door for stress to come in.

These three problems can affect us in a very significant way if we allow them to. They can adversely affect our lives physically, emotionally, and spiritually. Each one of them has the power to restrict and even ruin a person's life. Praise God though for the gospel! The good news Jesus brought to the world was,
"I came that they may have life, and have it abundantly."
(John 10:10b).

This, therefore, surely must mean a life without worry, fear and stress. How can we possibly enjoy the richness and fullness of abundant life in the way that the Bible speaks of, if we are troubled by any one of these things?

Through Christ's provision, then, we find the answer, but before we consider that let us look at four examples, two from the Old Testament, and two from the New, of people who lived with their hearts ruled by God's peace. Even though these people were in the most critical of circumstances they still remained totally secure.

(A) DAVID - 1 Samuel 17:41-51
Here we have a shepherd boy, destined to become King. It is worth reminding ourselves that at this stage in his development David was just

172

a young man, unlike the mature, hardened warriors that were accustomed to battle in the army of Israel. Yet even though these men were seasoned soldiers, not one of them had the courage to step forward and take on the giant Goliath.

This enemy of God's people was strutting up and down, making a mockery of Israel and also trying to make a fool of God, but no-one had the confidence to do anything about it. Therefore, this young lad steps forward, totally inexperienced, and in himself ill-equipped to do very much. As David approaches Goliath we first of all notice the tactic his enemy uses against him; it is the same strategy he employs against all of God's children.

The first thing Goliath does, having mocked and cursed David, is to try to sow insecurity into the heart of that godly man. He says to him,
".... Come to me, and I will give your flesh to the birds of the air and to the beasts of the field." (verse 44).
What a terrifying prospect! And let us not forget these were not empty words; this man was a giant, he had the wherewithal to carry through his threat.

Goliath was making a pronouncement over David's life; he was telling him what the outcome of his situation was going to be. This is exactly what Satan tries to do with us. He makes pronouncements over our lives personally, and states how our problems will unfold.

Someone ruled by the peace of God like David though, does not get trapped by such talk. He looks at Goliath and replies:
".... You come to me with a sword and with a spear and with a javelin; but I come to you in the name of the Lord of hosts, and the God of the armies of Israel." (verse 45).

David did not come against Goliath in the arrogance of youth, making all manner of wild boasts; his confidence was not in his own strength, but in God's. This is often the mistake we make and the reason why we struggle and fail in this area; simply because we try to take on our problems in our own ability and sort out our difficulties in our own strength. David though, shows us the right action to take. He immediately goes back to the source of his authority and strength in God, and he stands in the name of the Lord.

The next thing David does is very interesting; we don't often think of him prophesying, but that is exactly what he now does against Goliath. He says,

> *"This day the Lord will deliver you into my hand, and I will strike you down, and cut off your head; and I will give the dead bodies of the host of the Philistines this day to the birds of the air and to the wild beasts of the earth...."* (verse 46).

In taking such a stand David was assured of victory; Goliath did not stand a chance!

This is the most effective way to deal with the enemy. The only way to break any pronouncement from him over our life is to begin to declare the truth of what God says.

(B) ELISHA - 2 Kings 6:11-19

In this incident the prophet of God is in a very difficult situation. While Elisha is staying in the city with his servant, the king has sent out a great army to capture him. These soldiers come by night and completely surround the place where they are staying. When daybreak arrives the servant gets up, looks out of the window, and nearly has a heart-attack at what he sees! Talk about worry, fear and stress, this poor man has the lot! Full of anxious concern he cries out saying,

> *"Alas, my master! What shall we do?"* (verse 15b).

Elisha though, as cool as could be, turns round to his servant and says, *"Fear not, for those who are with us are more than those who are with them".* (verse 16). Here we notice that someone ruled by the peace of God views their problem from a spiritual perspective. They look with the eye of faith and see beyond their immediate predicament.

We come now to the second reason why we can struggle and lose our peace. It is because we look at our problems just from a natural point of view. When we only take a human perspective into account, we quickly get into trouble and the door to worry, fear and stress opens wide. Sometimes we see no further than the problems that are immediately confronting us. The first step to remaining in victory is to look beyond what we are facing in the natural, and see in the spirit, with the eye of faith, so that we look at the situation from God's point of view.

This is exactly what Elisha did, and why he remained confident. We notice also that he wanted his servant to experience the same peace he had, which is why he prayed,
"O Lord, I pray thee, open his eyes that he may see."
(verse 17a).

As soon as Elisha said this, the servant's eyes were opened, and then he saw the great host of the armies of heaven, encompassed about the enemy. They were there all the time, but only someone ruled by the peace of God can see that. This is because they are actually looking for the solution to come from God, rather than being focussed upon their problem.

(C) STEPHEN - Acts 6:8 - 7:60
Here we have a godly man, full of the Holy Spirit, being falsely accused before the religious leaders. People were saying things about him that were not true. They were manipulating the facts, and distorting the truth with the intention of putting him in a bad light. These men were even accusing him of speaking words of blasphemy and yet he was completely innocent.

You and I know how we feel when others say things about us that are not accurate. If people are stating that we have done things that we know we haven't, immediately we start to get defensive and agitated. We begin to feel the need to justify ourselves, stand up for our rights, and 'fight our corner.' Once we start to do this we open ourselves up to a great deal of tension and the first place it is usually seen is on our face. We begin to lose our sense of composure, and in its place come signs of anxiety and stress.

With this in mind, just look at the example we find here in Stephen. In spite of all these lies being spoken about him the scripture says,

"And gazing at him, all who sat in the council saw that his face was like the face of an angel." (verse 15).

What a wonderful picture of peace and security! The reason Stephen was able to be like this is, I believe, a great challenge to every Christian. What it demonstrates is that someone ruled by the peace of God actually believes God is still on the throne! They live as though God is for them, taking care of their life. Such people do not feel the need to justify themselves because they know God will vindicate them; they are not concerned about 'fighting their corner,' because they believe the battle is the Lord's!

It is very easy for us to talk and sing about the lordship of Jesus Christ, but this is never truly seen in our lives until we are going through difficult trials. It is when we can still remain calm and composed, because we know God is in control, that the reality of His lordship is expressed.

Stephen's situation gets much worse in Acts chapter 7. His accusers now want to kill him; they want this man out of the way. So with all the viciousness, hatred and strength they have, they begin to hurl stones against Stephen's face and body.

I cannot imagine more stressful circumstances to be in than that of being stoned to death, and yet as we look at Stephen we see something quite amazing. He has already taken the first step to keeping his peace because he,

".... gazed into heaven and saw the glory of God, and Jesus standing at the right hand of God." (verse 55).

The second step that he takes, though, is even more remarkable. Right in the midst of this incredibly stressful situation of being stoned to death, Stephen kneels down and in a loud voice prays,

"Lord, do not hold this sin against them...." (verse 60b).

We learn from this that someone ruled by the peace of God is more concerned about others than they are about themselves. This brings us to another major reason why we sometimes struggle in the area of worry, fear and stress. It is because we are too self-centred. When we are preoccupied, thinking about our problems, what people have done to us, how we are going to manage, and what others may think, then we have completely taken our eyes off God and focussed them on ourselves. The alternative is to direct our energy and concern outward, to the needs of others, even those who don't deserve it, just like Stephen did.

Imagine the difference it would make to our own lives, if rather than seething with anger and resentment towards those who have abused us, let us down, or in some way done us an injustice, we did what Stephen did and prayed for them. This is one of the reasons Jesus taught,

"…. Love your enemies and pray for those who persecute you." (Matthew 5:44).

When we do so, it releases all the tension and stress that builds up in us because of people's unjust and thoughtless actions.

(D) PAUL AND SILAS - Acts 16:23-26

These two disciples have been imprisoned for their faith and are suffering in very hard circumstances. There was nothing unusual about them being held in such a place, but on this occasion it is particularly difficult for them. They have just been very badly beaten up, put into stocks and placed in the inner prison cell. In spite of this awful predicament though, we see how someone ruled by the peace of God responds. In verse 25, it says,

"But about midnight Paul and Silas were praying and singing hymns to God….."

The passage indicates that what they were expressing was not merely a whimper, because it tells us that all the other prisoners heard them.

We learn from this that someone ruled by the peace of God responds to principles they know to be right, whether they feel pleasant or not. Here is another reason why we can struggle in the area of maintaining peace in our life; simply because we allow ourselves to be dictated to by our feelings.

With some Christians, if they don't feel like praising the Lord then they go quiet, and start to withdraw. When they don't feel like reading their Bibles or praying, they tend to put them to one side and wait until they feel a bit better. If they don't feel like going to the meeting one night, they will give it a miss, until the following week. This leads not only to very erratic Christian living, but also to an experience devoid of peace. If, however, we determine to do what we know is right, regardless of our feelings, we will find God's peace and be delivered from the emotional turmoil of our circumstances.

By proving God in such situations we place ourselves in a position where we can receive His blessing and grace. Having experienced this we are then also able to impart that grace to others who are struggling. When we go to encourage them, we will not be preaching a sermon at them, or simply passing on nice platitudes, rather we will be imparting life to them.

This is made clear in Philippians chapter 4 where Paul finds himself yet again in a prison cell. From this position he is writing to encourage other Christians to remain consistent and not to be governed by their feelings. What he has to say comes across with a certain ring of reality, because he has proved it in his own life. With words full of empathy and authority he writes,
> *"Rejoice in the Lord always; again I will say, Rejoice."*
>
> (verse 4).

Before further consideration is given to how we can possess peace in the midst of problems, we need to look again at the scripture we began with in Colossians 3:15. There it says *"Let the peace of Christ rule in your hearts ....."* This word *"Let...."* shows that we can help, or hinder the process. There is an abundance of God's peace always available to meet our every need, but we must allow that peace to rule within us. The way we do this is by following scriptural steps. Let us look at three of them:

178

Firstly,

CULTIVATE A CLOSE RELATIONSHIP WITH THE LORD

There can be no short cut taken here because God is the source of our peace. Therefore, if we have a weak relationship with Him, then this will be reflected in the measure of peace we have. If, however, we have a strong relationship like David, Elisha, Stephen and Paul, we will know a strong experience of His peace in our lives.

Jesus said,

> *"Peace I leave with you; my peace I give to you; not as the world gives do I give you."* (John 14:27a).

In this one statement, *".... not as the world gives..."* Jesus was saying that we can receive a measure of peace from the world, but what kind of peace is this? It is a peace that comes from alcohol, drugs, yoga, New Age teaching, Eastern Mysticism, breathing methods, relaxation tapes etc. The one thing we will always notice about this though, is that Jesus is always left out.

The peace of God, on the other hand, is quite different; without exception, Jesus is always the centre and the very substance of that peace. In Ephesians 2:14 we see that peace is not just a principle, it is a person. This is why it says,

> *"For He is our peace, who made us both one, and has broken down the dividing wall of hostility."*

Jesus has completely removed every barrier and obstacle that would stand between ourselves and God. Because of this, when we come on the basis of our relationship with Christ, we can approach Him with full assurance of faith, confident of receiving His grace to help in our time of need. In understanding that this peace is a person, we begin to realise the importance of building a close relationship with that person. Some aspects of doing so are:

(A) *Hard Work*

To cultivate a close relationship requires serious effort. It is true to say that in any marriage, if it is going to be successful, then from day one to the day we die, we have to work at it. The moment we start to take our partner granted and get a little casual or indifferent toward them, then we are heading for trouble. The same is true with God. A strong relationship with Him will involve 100% commitment. This is not striving after God, but rather an attitude of diligence, whole-heartedness, and a desire to give our very best at all times.

We cannot just sit back and expect God's peace to come. There can be no true peace for 'spiritual couch potatoes,' and in the Church today there are a lot of such people. Lazy and undisciplined Christians will not only have a weak relationship with God, they will also not know His peace in any lasting way. Release from worry, fear and stress becomes ours only as we seek after God with all of our heart. This is what David was expressing from his own experience when he said,
> *"I sought the Lord, and He answered me, and delivered me from all my fears."* (Psalm 34:4).

(B) *The Sacrifice Of Time*
Something that is basic to any relationship is the need to spend time with the other person. If we are so busy that there is little opportunity to really get to know them, then the relationship is going to be very shallow. This is vital also, as far as God is concerned, and especially so, in the rush and busyness of modern day life.

Very often people complain and make excuses by saying they lead extremely busy lives, with little time for themselves. While this is undoubtedly true for many people, the fact remains that we are the ones who govern our priorities and time. Not many people could have been busier than Jesus; no one had more demands made upon their time than the Lord did. Yet, in spite of this, we see His first priority was the relationship He had with God. The Bible records that,
> *"After He had dismissed the crowds, He went up on the mountain by Himself to pray."* (Matthew 14:23).

The word 'sacrifice' is never popular in the Christian vocabulary, which is why it needs to be understood within the context of a loving relationship. For example, if you remember your 'courting days,' you will recall then that no sacrifice was too great to make, or cost too much to give. Whatever it took, you just had to be with the person you loved.

While there might have been a sacrifice involved, it probably didn't really feel much like a sacrifice, because you wanted to do it.

The one thing we can be sure of is this; we will always find the time to do the thing that we want to do. It really comes down to a heart issue between ourselves and the Lord.

(C) *Loving Trust*

The foundation of any relationship is surely built on trust, especially in times of difficulty, and the only way that you can trust someone is when you are secure in their love for you. You are confident that they are not going to let you down, betray, abuse or intentionally hurt you in any way. When you are secure in their love, then it becomes natural and easy to trust them.

The importance of such love is vital, and its relevance in relation to trust is seen in the words,

> *"There is no fear in love, but perfect love casts out fear"*
> (1 John 4:18a).

When we are secure in the love of God, and we know that He is for us, that He will provide for our every need and will protect us, then all worry, fear and stress is driven out of our lives. We then become relaxed about trusting Him and simply rest, assured of His care.

Secondly, CONQUER THE BATTLE-GROUND OF THE MIND

Over ten years ago I can remember travelling the country speaking on the subject, *"Are you a warrior, or a worrier?"* It was very relevant then and certainly is still so today. The Church seems to be full of worriers. We can sing and read about overcoming and conquering, but if we cannot win the battle-ground of our own thought life then we are not going to get very far in this regard.

The vital area of the mind is addressed by Paul's words to the Romans when he says,

> *"Do not be conformed to this world but be transformed by the renewal of your mind...."* (Romans 12:2).

We see from this that we can be either *conformed* - that is, living just like everyone else, or we can be *transformed* - to be what the Bible says we can be. The major battle-ground that determines this is the area of our thought life.

Someone once said that when a Christian stays his mind on Christ, he develops a wonderful 'Calm-plex.' This is the promise given to us through the prophet Isaiah when he says,
> *"Thou dost keep him in perfect peace, whose mind is stayed on thee...."* (Isaiah 26:3).

If our mind is not *stayed* on God it becomes open to all manner of flash thoughts, coming from many different directions, and often when we least expect them. They are thoughts that 'pepper' our mind, trying to make us feel uneasy, anxious and troubled. These can be memories from the past, concerns about the present, or fears for the future.

Also, added to this is the very real problem that demons speak to our mind as well. The devil knows better than most Christians the power of the mind. He is only too aware that if he can build a stronghold in our thought life, then he can literally begin to control our actions.

The way he achieves this is quite simple. All he has to do is sow seed thoughts into our mind of doubt, resentment, suspicion, unbelief, lust etc. As we give them a second thought, they settle in our thinking; we turn them over in our minds, play them out in our imagination and eventually believe them. It is at this point that they become a stronghold that influences our actions. Thoughts also that are totally out of character for us like irrational, suicidal, reckless, and compulsive thoughts, very often have this demonic origin.

It is very important that we see **all** thoughts contrary to God's word for what they actually are. They are not just minor irritations; they are enemies to our victory, intent on disrupting our peace, damaging our potential and destroying our relationship with God. If we viewed them in this light, then we would take them more seriously and certainly act accordingly.

182

These thoughts are not just enemies to our victory though, they are also impostors, masquerading as fact and truth, but in reality are lies and distortions. They have no right to be there and can only remain in our lives, becoming strongholds controlling us, when we allow them to stay there. In giving them room, they become a fixed pattern of thinking, dictating our actions and disrupting our feelings.

One of the most effective weapons in winning this battle is to be proactive in our thinking and not just reactive. To be reactive is vital and powerful, but very often this is all we do, and it is only the first step to winning the complete battle.

Reactive thinking is seen in 2 Corinthians 10:5. Here Paul talks about the need to, *"Take every thought captive to obey Christ".* The thoughts that are contrary to God's word attack our mind, and we react to them by bringing them into obedience to the words of Jesus.

Victory in the thought life though, is not just a case of rejecting and throwing out all the rubbish, we must also continually fill our minds with that which is wholesome. Therefore, reactive thinking is taking action **when** we are attacked, but being pro-active, is taking action as a habit of life **before** that assault on our mind begins. It is cleansing and renewing our minds as a way of life, throughout the day.

This action is seen in the words of Paul when he says,
"Finally, brethren, whatever is true, whatever is honourable, whatever is just, whatever is pure, whatever is lovely, whatever is gracious, if there is any excellence, if there is anything worthy of praise, think about these things. What you have learned and received and heard and seen in me, do; and the God of peace will be with you."
(Philippians 4:8&9).

We see from this that when we are actively playing our part and taking responsibility for renewing our minds, then God promises to fulfil His commitment to us by maintaining peace in our life.

One other scripture that speaks about proactive thinking is found in Colossians 3:1&2. Paul says,

"If then you have been raised with Christ, seek the things that are above, where Christ is, seated at the right hand of God. Set your minds on things that are above, not on things that are on earth."

Here Paul emphasises the importance of the things we set our minds on. We must take care not to set our minds on the ungodly philosophies, standards and values of this world. Most Christians would say they never allow their minds to be occupied with such things, and yet sit for hours watching television programmes like Brookside, East Enders, Coronation Street, Emmerdale etc.

I don't believe there is anything wrong in watching a 'Soap,' but there is something seriously wrong if our mind is *set* on these things, so that we get frantic and uptight if we think we are going to miss an episode. I've known conflict caused in the homes of some Christians, simply because someone had forgotten to make the 'necessary' recording. I was stating this very point at a meeting recently when, all of a sudden from the back of the church, a lady stood up and shouted out, *"That's exactly what happened in our home this evening!"*

Thirdly, **CHOOSE ALWAYS THE RIGHTEOUS ALTERNATIVE**
    When we do not make this choice, at all times, then we immediately lose our peace. Sin will always destroy peace. Throughout the day, from when we wake up to when we go to sleep, we are making choices between right and wrong, good and evil, God's will and our will. It is the choices we make that determine the quality of life we have.

What is important to recognise is that other people cannot determine the quality of our life, nor can our circumstances; the choices *we* make decide this. The example of Paul's commitment to making righteous choices show clearly how they affected his life. Even though he was often in surroundings of hardship, and frequently in pain, inflicted upon him by others, still he could say,

*" .... I have learned, in whatever state I am to be content. I
know how to be abased, and I know how to abound...."*
(Philippians 4:11&12).

One of the most thought-provoking passages in the Bible, that
refers to the need and consequence of making right choices, is found in
the words of Moses when he addressed Israel. He said,

*"I call heaven and earth to witness against you this day,
that I have set before you life and death, blessing and curse;
therefore choose life, that you and your descendants may
live..."* (Deuteronomy 30:19).

Moses understood the importance for Israel to make righteous
choices and so he urged them to do so by saying, *"Therefore choose
life, that you might live...."* The only way that we can truly *live*, is
when we are choosing the life and blessing of God. When we do not,
then what we are actually doing, by default, is choosing death, and a
curse upon ourselves. There can be no neutral position as far as God is
concerned. The devil always has an open door into our lives when we
do not make righteous choices.

I have used the words *"choose"* and *"alternative"* deliberately,
because it is necessary to see that there is always an alternative to the
unrighteous attitude, thought, word and action, and it is our
responsibility as an act of our will to choose it. An example of this is
seen in 1 Corinthians 10:13, when Paul says,

*"God is faithful, and He will not let you be tempted
beyond your strength, but with the temptation will also
provide the way of escape."* - (**the alternative**).

We must not only see the alternative; we have to choose to take it.
Again, another example of this can be found in the words of Jesus, when
He was addressing the whole problem of anxiety and worry in Matthew
6:25-34. Here, He gives a list of things not to worry about. Jesus
instructs His disciples not to worry about food, drink, clothing, or even
the cares of tomorrow. Then, having said this, He gives the alternative
to choose which is,

"Seek first His Kingdom and His righteousness, and all these things shall be yours as well." (verse 33).

Probably over 90% of all our problems and battles with stress come because of unrighteous attitudes. Wherever we express negativity, anger, resentment, selfishness, independence, pride, criticism etc. then this builds up stress in our lives. If, however, we will be prepared in every situation always to choose the righteous alternative, then this would bring immediate release from the yoke of pressure that we bring ourselves under, through unrighteousness.

For example, rather than reacting to a situation of offence with resentment, we choose the righteous option of forgiveness. Instead of criticism, we choose encouragement. As an alternative to being negative, we choose always to speak positively. Rather than being selfish we choose to be thoughtful and considerate. Instead of a proud attitude we choose the righteous alternative of humility. Each time we make the decision to do this we are actually choosing the life and blessing of God.

The Lord's will for us, therefore, is that we live with His peace ruling in our hearts. We can know peace in the midst of problems as we: *Firstly*, Cultivate a close relationship with the Lord. *Secondly*, Conquer the battle-ground of the mind and, *Thirdly*, Choose always the righteous alternative, in every situation.

Conclusion

Greatness in God's sight is within your grasp. In reading this book I trust you have been challenged and encouraged to see this and are ready to live in the good of it.

A man by the name of Roberto C. Goizueta rose from the ranks of ordinary working men to become president of the Coca Cola Company, one of the world's largest business enterprises. His favourite saying was from the Japanese writer Xishima: *"To know and not to act is not yet to know"*. He made this the guiding principle of his life and we could not conclude with any better counsel. What we now know we must act upon.

We have seen how God has a destiny for each of us and that it can be fulfilled, not in our own strength, but by the power of His Holy Spirit at work within us. If we are prepared to act upon what we have learned, and pay the cost of what His word demands, then we can be among those who are making history and not just reading about it.

Everything comes down to our relationship with the Lord and how high a value we place upon realising our full potential, for His glory.

Years ago a young black child was growing up in Cleveland, in a home which he later described as *"materially poor, but spiritually rich"*.

One day a famous athlete, by the name of Charlie Paddock, came to his school to speak to the students. At the time Paddock was considered 'The fastest human being alive'. He told the children, *"Listen! What do you want to be? You name it and believe that God will help you be it."*

That little boy decided that he too wanted to be the fastest human being on earth and he went to his track coach and told him of his dream. His coach said to him, *"It's great to have a dream, but to attain your dream you must build a ladder to it. This is the ladder to your dream:*

*The first rung is **determination!** And the second is **dedication!** The third rung is **discipline!** And the fourth rung is **attitude!**"*

The result of all that motivation is that the young child went on to win four gold medals in the 1936 Berlin Olympics. He won the 100 meter dash and broke the Olympic and world records for the 200 meter. One of his records lasted for twenty-four years, and his name was Jesse Owens.

Having decided what you want to be, may God grant you His help as you seek to realise your full potential?

Other Publications By Yan Hadley

Available From
New Life In Christ Ministries
45 Heatherbrook Road
Leicester
LE4 1AL

Telephone : 0116 235 6992
E-mail:NLICM@hadleyl.freeserve.co.uk

REAPING GOD'S HARVEST
(Equipping the Church For Evangelism)

Yan's aim in this book is to stimulate faith in the lives of every believer to discover the ability of sharing Christ with others. Through clear practical teaching and personal illustrations evangelism is seen to be, not only a responsibility, but also a privilege and joy.

ANSWERING TODAY'S PROBLEMS
(Helping Ourselves to Help Others)

This books shows clearly God's answer to some common problems in life today. People will find help not only for themselves, but also insight into being able to help others.

CONSISTENT CHRISTIAN LIVING
(Four Keys To Remaining In Victory)

Many Christians find it difficult to accept that they can live consistently with joy, fulfilment and victory. In this book Yan writes to lift the expectancy of every believer to think differently. A life of consistency is seen to be normal and not merely for a select few.

Why Not Visit Our Website: www.eclipse.co.uk/imagemakers/newlife